Dr. Friedhelm Mühleib

Vitamins for fitness, health and beauty

A practical guide to:

- planning your vitamin intake
- your personal vitamin profile
- vitamin-rich meals for everyday eating

Important

The views expressed by the authors of the HEALTH CARE
TODAY series may differ at times from generally recognized
orthodox medicine. All readers must decide for themselves
whether, and to what extent, they wish to follow the advice
given in this book.

Any form of self-treatment demands a high degree of
responsibility on the part of the individual. Before
commencing any treatment, please make sure you have read
and understood the advice that has been given. It is also
important to stress that seemingly mild ailments may
sometimes conceal serious illnesses which should be treated
by a qualified medical practitioner. If you are uncertain
about the cause or progress of an illness, always consult
your doctor. Do not take risks – when in doubt, always go to
the doctor.

Contents

Foreword

Are vitamins some kind of wonder drug?

More is required and expected of vitamins than of almost any other food substance. For most of us, vitamins stand for health, energy, activity and resilience. They are thought to brighten our mood and improve concentration. Some people even expect them to perform miracles in the fight against diseases such as cancer, heart attacks or rheumatism.

Our expectations of what vitamins can do are probably far from realistic. After all, how much do we actually know about vitamins? Not enough, in all probability! Our views on vitamins and what is meant by an adequate vitamin intake is often fairly ill-defined. We know that fruit and vegetables are rich in vitamins, but when asked which fruits and vegetables are good sources of which vitamin, most of us have no idea.

Everyone is familiar with vitamin C, of course. However, as many of the activities of all the other vitamins are frequently ascribed to vitamin C, our faith in it is often excessive. If our knowledge of the other vitamins is very sketchy then many vitamin sources, which are just as important for our health as fruit and vegetables, will be unfamiliar, undervalued, and may even be excluded altogether from our diet.

Our readiness to reach for the vitamin bottle is another indication of how much we expect of vitamins. Listless, tired, exhausted, stressed? Vitamin deficiency provides a convenient explanation in all these cases.

How many people know their vitamin requirement?

Vitamin preparations

When it comes to an understanding of our own personal requirements, there are quite a number of things we need to know before we can decide whether we are in need of additional vitamins: Are we getting enough vitamins from the food we eat? Does our current state of health, or our lifestyle expose us to particular stress factors which increase our vitamin requirement? Which foods do we need to eat to improve our intake of a particular vitamin?

Risk factors influence the amount we require

Questions of this type are almost impossible to answer without the help of experts.

Our vitamin intake is generally good

The average person today has a good vitamin intake. True vitamin-deficiency diseases such as rickets, scurvy and pellagra were eliminated in this country many years ago. Where the problem exists at all it is a matter rather of uncertainty as to whether the body's vitamin requirement is being met in specific risk groups, than of true vitamin deficiency. On the other hand, it is becoming clear from many different investigations that there are also 'high-risk vitamins', where hardly anyone receives the optimum quantity.

High-risk groups; high-risk vitamins

Recent research into vitamins has shown that our present-day knowledge is far from complete. The finding that vitamins A, C and E very probably help prevent certain types of cancer, myocardial infarction and rheumatism is one of the most exciting discoveries to date.

This guide tells you more about this and answers commonly asked questions such as: How can we know if we lack a particular vitamin? Can vitamins really protect us from cancer, heart attacks and other Western diseases? Should we take vitamin pills, and if so, does it make any difference whether these are natural vitamins obtained from foods, or synthetic substitutes?

Vitamins prevent disease

You will also find practical hints on how you can optimise your vitamin intake, and how to avoid vitamin loss. You can discover whether you belong to a high-risk group, and what is meant by the expression 'vitamin depleters'. There are also brief summaries of all vitamins and their functions. These include an account of deficiency symptoms, our requirement of each vitamin and the amount present in foods as well as the use of vitamins in the field of medicine.

In addition to information about the beneficial, health-giving properties of vitamins, this book also contains a series of exquisitely beautiful photomicrographs taken at 450x magnification.

Vitamins keep our bodies in working order

What are vitamins?

Vitamin is a compound word made up of two Latin words: 'vita', meaning life and 'amin', meaning 'contains nitrogen'. Funk, the scientist who coined the term 'vitamin' as early as 1911, believed that all vitamins were nitrogen-containing substances essential to life.

We now know that Funk was wrong in his first assumption that all vitamins were nitrogen-containing. Although vitamins are all similar in their activity, mediating important chemical metabolic reactions in the body in their capacity as controllers and regulators, chemically they are utterly different substances with very few similarities or related characteristics.

However, Funk was right about vitamins being organic compounds which are needed by the body for all its vital functions.

Many primitive organisms still retain the capacity to manufacture vitamins, but we humans have gradually lost this ability as we have evolved. Many vitamins cannot be manufactured by our own biochemical processes, while others often cannot be made in sufficient quantities. This means that we have to ingest vitamins as essential nutrients from our food. The complete lack of even a single vitamin in our diet for any significant period of time leads to deficiency phenomena which can, in time, lead to death.

There are now known to be 13 major vitamins. Historically these have been classified in simple alphabetical order. But this way of naming individual vitamins, using letters sometimes accompanied by numbers, is non-scientific and can lead to confusion. For example, vitamin B is actually a group of vitamins rather than a single vitamin and whilst we have vitamins B1, B2, B6 and B12, vitamins B3, B4 or B7 do not exist.

Vitamins ensure the correct functioning of the metabolism

Vitamins are important lubricants

Metabolism is our engine, and the fuel which it converts into energy is the food that we eat. All engines need lubrication if they are to function smoothly, and vitamins are some of the most important lubricants available to our metabolism.

The elements that make up the metabolism are the ingestion of food and production of energy to form the body's constituents, and the elimination of waste material. The metabolism controls the lifelong cycle of formation, re-organisation and breakdown of the body's cells, and regulates the growth, development and ageing processes of the body. However, metabolism does more than simply programme the long-term processes of life and development. It also ensures that all operational processes of the body are functioning correctly. It provides the energy for the bellows action of the lungs, the beating of the heart, and the silent, continuous functioning of all other organs. It does these things by providing the energy-consuming systems of the body with a constant supply of fuel and active substances from digestion. These fuels are normally contained in the food we eat. They are classified as follows:

Fuels from food

- Energy-supplying nutrients (all substances containing calories)
    - Protein
    - Fat
    - Carbohydrates
- Active substances (nutrients which do not supply energy)
    - Vitamins
    - Minerals
    - Trace elements
- Water, the medium without which the metabolism and the vital processes in the body will not take place.

Minerals, trace elements and vitamins are the active substances needed by the metabolism if the energy-supplying nutrients, protein, fat and carbohydrates are to be catabolized efficiently. Their function is comparable to that of engine lubricants. Many biochemical reactions take place only in the presence of certain minerals and vitamins which, as constituents of enzymes are mediators, catalysts or initiators of the reactions from which the body ultimately creates its vital energy.

Vitamins are important active substances

In terms of its constituent materials, the body is nothing but a nutrient store. It consists of 15-20% protein, 4-6% fat, 1% carbohydrates and 4-5% minerals and trace elements. The remaining 65-70% is water.

Vitamins account for an insignificant proportion of the weight, with the body's total vitamin reserve amounting to only a few grams, but these are essential for the body's survival.

How much does a person need?

'A person who is getting sufficient vitamin C and other vitamins can prolong his or her life span and period of good health by an estimated 25 years.' This statement was made by Linus Pauling, winner of the Nobel prize for chemistry. Pauling, who when he was in his late nineties still had spectacularly good health, credited it to taking huge doses of vitamins every day.

Experts still have conflicting ideas regarding the actual quantities of vitamins a person needs. In 1991, the Department of Health report on Health and Social Subjects (No. 41) included a section on 'Dietary Reference Values for Food Energy & Nutrients for the UK'. This shows clearly that our Recommended Daily Amount (RDA) was not sufficient. The report suggested new guidelines using new terminology: Reference Nutrient Intake (RNI). This is the amount of nutrient which is sufficient to meet the needs of 97% of the population. Although it is roughly equivalent to the old RDA, the RNI level provides a lot of people with more than they actually need.

Our daily requirement of many vitamins is still under debate

There is quite a difference between the requirement and the recommended amount. For example, the recommended daily amount for vitamin C is for 75mg per day – roughly the amount contained in a large orange. Linus Pauling took up to 15g of vitamin C every day to maintain health, an amount that is 1000 times greater than the RDA. However, 10-15mg of vitamin C per day is sufficient to prevent visible deficiency phenomena and 20-25mg is enough to ensure optimal wound repair – a process which does not function without this vitamin.

The RDA far exceeds the requirement

What these figures reveal is that the recommended daily amounts are usually far higher than the physical requirement, which is nothing more than the minimum quantity of a vitamin that needs to be ingested in order to prevent deficiency phenomena occurring.

Although apparently clear, this definition becomes extremely complex when it is a matter of an exact specification of such minute quantities of a vitamin. Another reason for the difficulty is that the vitamin requirement varies from one individual to another.

Influencing factors

Individual vitamin requirements depend, among other things, on the following factors:
• The metabolism – the absorption of vitamins from food, the body's reserves, and the utilization and excretion of vitamins are all highly individual. Vitamin utilization in the metabolism is more efficient in some people than in others.
• Personal circumstances influence a person's vitamin requirement. Anyone who is suffering from stress or has a very physically demanding job, such as labouring, or who smokes or drinks alcohol will have a higher vitamin requirement.
• High-risk groups include pregnant or breast-feeding women, infants, adolescents, the elderly and people who are sick and have a higher than average vitamin requirement (High-risk groups, page 87).

Calculating the requirement

To help determine the actual requirement, scientists have produced skilfully devised analytical methods. For most vitamins, however, even these cannot result in exact requirement values, for the reasons already stated.

Measurable
in blood

Notwithstanding attempts to identify requirements and detect deficiencies by measuring the concentration of the vitamin in the blood, these two parameters are difficult to define. Even so, the vitamin content of the blood can be used to differentiate between high and moderate risk, and to validate your vitamin intake.

If you think you could be suffering from a vitamin deficiency, you should speak to your doctor about the possibility of having your vitamin status determined. If the doctor shares your concern, the vitamin intake, or the vitamin content of your blood serum, can be measured by performing the appropriate analysis. Unfortunately, these analyses are laborious and expensive and the results are often inconclusive. The better alternative is to prevent deficiency or low vitamin intake by eating a nutritious and varied diet.

If deficiency
is suspected,
the vitamin
status can be
measured

Things you should know about "recommended dietary allowances":
Guidelines on eating for vitamin intake are only intended as a way of giving people some indication of how much of each vitamin should be included in their diet. They may be helpful when planning your diet or when assessing a deficiency. However, if a deficiency is suspected the actual intake status will need to be measured using biochemical methods. For the average person the recommended allowance usually exceeds the actual requirement by quite large amounts. The Department of Health recommendations always include a wide margin of safety which is added to the assumed requirement in order to safeguard the intake of high-risk groups. The recommended allowances need not be subdivided into uniform daily doses. It is quite sufficient to balance your vitamin intake on a weekly basis.

Vitamin
balance

You can use the test in the next chapter to find out whether you are receiving sufficient vitamins each day.

Your personal vitamin profile

Are you getting enough vitamin C? Do you often feel weary and lacking in energy? Do you need to take medication on a regular basis? Are you breast-feeding? Are you permanently stressed out?

How well your body is supplied with vitamins depends on three factors: the food you eat, your current state of health, and your lifestyle or personal circumstances. The test below will provide you with the opportunity to examine these areas in your own life. You will discover whether your personal eating pattern means that you are getting too little of some vitamins, or whether, on account of your lifestyle, you need more vitamins than you have been getting in your food up to now. On the other hand, you may find that you are getting an optimum supply of all vitamins.

The correct answers can be found on pages 14 and 15. From these you will learn whether your vitamin balance is essentially all right, whether it could be improved, or whether you should be seriously concerned about it.

This test is designed to ascertain your individual vitamin intake. All symptoms due to a vitamin deficiency may also be signs of other nutrient deficiencies or of acute or chronic disease. However, vitamins always play a crucial role in the combined action of all nutrients and their importance in maintaining the health of the body.

Nutrition

How frequently do you eat fresh fruit and vegetables, and how often do you drink juices prepared from fruit or vegetables?

☐ A daily   ☐ B less than three times a week

Are wholemeal bread, muesli and cereal dishes a regular part of your diet (more than twice a week)?

☐ A yes   ☐ B no

Do you dress salads with cold-pressed vegetable oils, and do you enjoy eating nuts or sunflower seeds?

☐ A yes   ☐ B no

Are you a vegetarian, and do you not have any fish, eggs, dairy produce or milk in your diet?
☐ A no   ☐ B yes

Do you enjoy liver, eating it at least once a month?
☐ A yes   ☐ B no

How often do you eat carrots and green vegetables, for example peas, broccoli and green cabbage?
☐ A three times   ☐ B very rarely
       a week

Do you season your food with large quantities of fresh or deep-frozen herbs?
☐ A always   ☐ B only use dried herbs

How often do you eat fast foods instead of meals which are rich in vegetables and green salad?
☐ A rarely   ☐ B at least three times a week

Do you often eat meat dishes in the canteen at work or in restaurants?
☐ A no/rarely   ☐ B yes

Are you able to resist sweets or cream cakes?
☐ A yes   ☐ B no

Health

Do you suffer from varicose veins or cellulite?
☐ A no   ☐ B yes

Do you tire easily; do you suffer from nervousness and lack of concentration?
☐ A rarely   ☐ B frequently

Have you been diagnosed as having an iron deficiency?
☐ A no   ☐ B yes

Do you need to use laxatives?
☐ A no   ☐ B yes

Do you take medication on a regular basis?
☐ A no   ☐ B yes

Do you succumb to every cold and bouts of 'flu?
☐ A no   ☐ B yes, often

Lifestyle and personal circumstances

Are you on the contraceptive pill?
☐ A no   ☐ B yes

Are you often upset or unstable for no apparent reason?
☐ A no   ☐ B yes, frequently

Have you just become pregnant, or are you breast-feeding?
☐ A no   ☐ B yes

How often do you drink alcohol (beer, wine or spirits)?
☐ A occasionally   ☐ B regularly

Do you smoke more than 6 cigarettes a day?
☐ A no   ☐ B yes

Are you always dieting?
☐ A no   ☐ B yes

Are you under 18 years of age?
☐ A no   ☐ B yes

Your test result

Now add up the number of times you ticked response A, and the number of times you ticked response B, and read your result assessment:

If you ticked A 15-22 times

If you have achieved the maximum score, you are obviously a person with an extraordinarily healthy lifestyle. You are well aware of the importance of vitamins, and you know which foods they can be found in. You are probably also very conscious of what you eat – you stick to low-calorie foods containing very little fat and you avoid sweet things. At home, fruit and vegetables are served up regularly, prepared in a variety of different ways. Your diet is balanced, and you get a good supply of all vitamins. Even if you are a little bit naughty once in a while, when you get very little in the way of vitamins, this does not directly imply that you are damaging your health. In the case of some vitamins, the body is able to fall back on its own reserves.

The basic rule is that the vitamin balance must be correct on a week-by-week basis.

If you ticked A 5–14 times

The way you are eating could easily lead you into a state of vitamin deficiency. If you belong to a high-risk group (you can read about these on page 87), this can increase the danger of a poor vitamin status still further. Do you often feel unwell without an obvious cause; does a decline in resilience sometimes mean that you find everyday life difficult; do you easily become nervous and impatient, and do you often have difficulty concentrating? Before these possible first signs of vitamin deficiency develop into clear symptoms, you should review your everyday eating habits and identify any weaknesses in your vitamin intake.

Supplement the food you eat with fresh juices (vitamin C), milk, dairy products and wholemeal products (vitamins B1, B2, biotin and niacin), eat mixed salads daily (vitamins A, C and K, and folic acid) dressed with cold-pressed vegetable oil (vitamin E), serve up tasty vegetable dishes and every now and then a piece of meat or fish (vitamins B6 and D). Seasonal fruits and a handful of nuts are rich in vitamins and will give you renewed vigour. Recommended dietary allowances can be found in the section on individual vitamins starting on page 49.

If you have ticked A 5 times or less

If you have ticked response A fewer than 5 times you are possibly already suffering from a deficiency of a number of vitamins; such deficiencies can seriously damage your health. Do not allow this to happen. Consult your doctor to find out what you can do to eliminate this deficiency as quickly as possible.

The first important step is to change your diet and possibly your lifestyle. However, a deficient vitamin intake cannot be compensated for fast enough by these means alone. A vitamin supplement may be required in these circumstances as a supplementary first-aid measure. Your doctor will be able to advise you on which one would be the most suitable for you.

Vitamin deficiencies occur gradually

You do not need to worry about the possibility of a vitamin deficiency simply because your daily food intake falls short of the recommended vitamin requirement. On the other hand, do not let the wide margins of safety included in the recommended allowances lead you to neglect the variety and volume of your vitamin intake. This could lead to malnutrition.

When a particular food is listed as containing a specific amount of a vitamin, this does not mean that this quantity is still present in the food after preparation, or that it is available to the metabolism.

Vitamin losses must be included in the calculation

• Many of the figures relate to fresh, raw, un-processed produce. Effects such as light, oxygen, heat (braising, boiling, baking or roasting), mincing or peeling reduce the vitamin content enormously.

Antivitamins

• Also present in the food we eat are substances which counteract the effects of vitamins. Known as antivitamins, these substances either render a particular vitamin chemically inactive or block its uptake into the body. Eggs provide one known example: although eggs are rich in biotin, raw eggs contain avidin, a chemical substance which actually inactivates the vitamin.

• Other vitamins present in certain foods are chemically bound to other substances, as a result they can no longer be taken up into the body. An example is niacin, which is present in cereal in a compound that cannot be digested.

Variable utilisation

• Sometimes the lack of other nutrients can impair or prevent the utilization of vitamins. One example is beta-carotene, the precursor of vitamin A found in vegetables, whose take up is greatly reduced if the vegetable is prepared in the total absence of fat – for example when it is eaten raw. This problem is easily solved with a few drops of oil.

For all these reasons it seems advisable to allow ourselves to be guided by the recommended allowances and, in the interests of our health, to ensure that our vitamin intake is optimised. For vitamin deficiencies do not happen overnight like a bout of 'flu: rather, they creep up on us almost unnoticed.

Development and manifestation of deficiencies

If the intake of a vitamin falls below the required level, the first thing to happen is that the vitamin reserves become depleted. How long these reserves last varies from one individual to another, according to the storage capacity of the body for the vitamin in question.

Blood values indicate the intake status

If the reserves are exhausted, the vitamin concentration in the blood falls. These low blood values are the first sign for clinicians of imminent deficiency. At this stage your personal well-being may still be completely normal, although tiredness, fatigue and poor concentration may be the first subjective warning signs.

Eventually, the vitamin content of the blood falls so low that the vitamins can no longer fully perform their functions as controlling and regulating substances in the metabolism. This results in a decline in the production of vitamin-dependent enzymes, proteins and hormones. The World Health Organization (WHO) has designated this situation as early-stage deficiency.

The first clinical symptoms to appear are usually non-specific, but even so they frequently cause a deterioration in the health of the individual. In vitamin K deficiency the clotting time of the blood is prolonged; if vitamin D is deficient, the calcium content of bone is reduced, and if the deficiency is in vitamin C, resistance to infection is impaired and wound repair is delayed.

Only at this stage do the characteristic vitamin deficiency diseases arise. Vitamin B12 deficiency is manifested as the complete clinical picture of pernicious anaemia, vitamin C deficiency as scurvy, vitamin B1 deficiency as beriberi, and vitamin D deficiency as rickets. Moreover, these disease manifestations cannot be reversed completely by rapid administration of the corresponding vitamins.

Deficiency diseases must be treated immediately

The end stage of vitamin deficiency is associated with irreversible deficiency symptoms. If left untreated, all vitamin deficiency is ultimately fatal; vitamins are absolutely essential for life.

Duration periods of the body's vitamin reserves	
Vitamin B12	3-5 years
Vitamin A	0-1 year
Folic acid	3-4 months
Vitamin C, niacin	cannot be stored
Vitamin B2, vitamin B6	2-6 weeks
Vitamin K	cannot be stored
Vitamin B1 (thiamine)	1-2 weeks

Low intake and its causes

The classic deficiency diseases, such as scurvy, have all but died out in countries like ours. In the developing world, however, the situation is completely different; there, vitamin deficiency is widespread and, together with undernourishment, leads to infections and disease, and thus hundreds of thousands of deaths.

Prosperity does not rule out deficiency disease

In industrialised countries we tend to see it in the form of inadequate intake and its potential consequences. The symptoms of this situation are exploited again and again in advertisements for vitamin products: 'Do you constantly feel tired, weary or unable to concentrate? Do you suffer from stress or fatigue? The reason could be a vitamin deficiency.' In the search to explain vague symptoms, a diagnosis of vitamin deficiency has often been leapt upon as a ready answer.

Whether, and if so to what extent, systemic disorders of this type can be attributable to low vitamin intake has still not been clarified scientifically. However, a link to low vitamin intake cannot be excluded in many cases, even if the symptoms can often be traced back to other causes. Nutritional physiologists have demonstrated through psychometric tests in the elderly that old people with low intake values came across in the tests as being more nervous, depressed and tired than did age-matched individuals with an adequate vitamin intake. Their underlying mood was worse, they were more agitated, and their short-

A link to low vitamin intake cannot be excluded

18

term memory and attentiveness were inferior to those in the control group, who were adequately supplied with vitamins.

Some reasons for low vitamin intake or vitamin deficiency

• Undernourishment and malnutrition – these usually only exist in developing countries.

• Maldigestion – in this disorder nutrients can no longer be properly released from the food. It occurs in people suffering from coeliac disease (systemic digestive disturbance) or mucoviscidosis (general disturbance of glandular secretions).

Diseases • Liver diseases often lead to a dramatic lowering of vitamin reserves; the reason for this is that the liver stores many vitamins and if it is diseased it can no longer fulfil this function.

• Inclusion in a population subgroup with elevated vitamin   Risk groups
uptake:children and adolescents, pregnant and breast-feeding women, the elderly (see High-risk groups, page 87).

• Infections aggravate pre-existing negative imbalances. Conversely, these imbalances – particularly those for vitamins A and C – in many cases give rise to infection. Susceptibility to infection increases because vitamin deficiency impairs antibody production, the formation of auxiliary agents of the immune system such as, for example lysosomal enzymes, and the resistance of many tissues, especially the skin and mucosae.

• Long-term antibiotic therapy, the contraceptive pill or anticonvulsants may trigger vitamin deficiencies or
Drugs aggravate a pre-existing slightly inadequate intake.

Vitamins from the pharmacist

For many people, reaching for the vitamin bottle is the obvious way to protect themselves from the consequences of vitamin deficiency, or even simply of low vitamin intake. Of course, everyone knows that their physical requirement can also be met by eating a varied and nutritious diet, but

not many of us relish the thought of assuming the arduous
task of calculating day by day whether our vitamin intake is
properly balanced. Finally, we are no doubt aware of our
highly individual weaknesses where eating is concerned,
whether this constitutes an inability to resist sweets and
confectionery or a passion for fast food. Another universally
known fact is that bad eating is usually associated with
vitamin deficiency. For this reason, many people prefer to
take vitamins pills just as a precaution.

Just how much is spent on vitamin tablets for self-
medication purposes is revealed in the sales figures.
Pharmacies turn over more than £65 million each year from
the sale of vitamin preparations. It is estimated that 80% of
these are taken purely for prophylactic purposes.
Furthermore, vitamin products are among the 15 best-
selling drug groups sold in pharmacies, though these figures
do not include the large number of products sold over-the-
counter in health food and chemist shops, and the health-
product section of retail outlets.

Presentations and effects

There is a whole series of reasons to justify taking a vitamin
product. Essentially, these are the same as the factors cited
as the cause of potential deficiency: inclusion in a high-risk
group, malnutrition or undernourishment, illness,
convalescence, chronic drug use, and prevention of certain
diseases, particularly cancer. If one of these reasons applies
in your case, you should select your product with care.

Vitamin products are now available in the form of tablets,
sugar-coated tablets, effervescent tablets, chews, syrup or
drops, and they come in all possible dosage forms. In
addition to single vitamin products, which contain only one
vitamin, there are also numerous multivitamins, no two of
which have exactly the same composition. Either ask your
doctor which product is most suitable for you, or make sure
you examine the contents and directions for use. Those
products containing up to a maximum of ten times the
recommended daily amount (RNI) are considered safe .
One of the problems with higher vitamin dosages is that

therapeutic activity is expressed (that means the vitamin acts like a drug). Secondly, with certain vitamins there is the risk of possible overdosage, with effects which are harmful to health.

As a rule, the vitamin content of over-the-counter drugs contains less than 10 times the recommended dose. Here too, the exception proves the rule. For example, vitamin E products are available in a dose of 200mg per sugar-coated tablet, the recommended dosage being one to be taken three times a day. Compare this with the recommended daily amount of 12mg! Problems arise when more than one product is taken simultaneously, in that particular care should be taken to ensure that the dose of each individual vitamin remains within the guidelines.

It is important to make allowance for the composition of any other drugs taken simultaneously. Drugs containing megadoses of vitamin B are prescribed for certain nervous disorders, and high-dose vitamin A products are used in the treatment of certain diseases of the eyes. Under no circumstances should supplementary vitamin B or vitamin A in the form of vitamin products be taken in such cases.

The best way to ensure a vitamin intake which can sustain health in the long-term is by eating the right sort of food. After all, it is quite possible for a well-balanced diet to contain amounts of individual vitamins corresponding to their recommended daily dose. On page 98 you will be able to find out how you can be sure of your vitamin intake by eating varied and healthy food, removing the need for all these calculations.

Are natural vitamins better than synthetic?

If there is a good reason for you having to take some form of vitamin preparations as a supplement, it is important that you always choose ones that are as natural as possible. As with every chemical substance that is associated with food, there is a large amount of controversy surrounding the advantages and disadvantages of synthetically produced vitamins.

It is, however, important to realise that today all vitamin

Almost all vitamins can be manufactured

supplements (with the exception of vitamin B12) are mass-produced by the pharmaceutical industry. The only truly 'natural' vitamins are those obtained from natural raw materials without chemical modification. However, to give the illusion of naturalness marketing strategists have coined a whole range of descriptive terms.

• 'Produced from natural raw materials' means that the vitamins were originally obtained from a foodstuff using chemical auxiliary agents, and then made into the preparation after further processing. Pure vitamin E can be extracted from wheat-germ and then converted into a capsule-ready form.

• 'With natural vitamin' usually means that a preparation is supplemented with small quantities of vitamins obtained from vegetables or oil-seed. This is essentially for no other reason than the selling power of that little word 'natural'.

But what anyone buying these products needs to know is: are natural vitamins more effective than synthetic ones? The answer to this question is, perhaps surprisingly, 'no'. Whether a vitamin is artificially manufacturered or not is irrelevant to the way it is used within the body. Take vitamin C as an example. The chemical name for vitamin C is ascorbic acid, but whether the absorbic acid or vitamin C was obtained from plants or synthesised in the laboratory makes absolutely no difference to its activity within the human body.

Equal in their activity

A varied intake of essential elements is crucial

Unlikely as it may seem, synthetic vitamins frequently do better than those ingested with food; this is because foods often contain other factors which are an obstacle to the use of a vitamin. However, this is not intended to devalue the provision of vitamins from the diet. After all, vitamins in wholefoods are surrounded by many other nutrients which we need if we are to stay healthy and well nourished.

Megadoses – more does not always mean better

Some readers will no doubt respond to the warnings against excessively large vitamin doses with scepticism. Look at the example set by Linus Pauling (page 9) who took vastly increased doses of vitamin C every day. It may be that Pauling was only able to survive such large doses because he had been blessed with an especially robust constitution. For it is a proven fact that, without exception, more does not always mean better.

In the first instance, the positive action of a vitamin can be potentiated by increasing the dose. But as soon as this dose exceeds the normal range, the vitamin is no longer a nutrient, but a pharmacologically-active substance. The body attempts to deal with this huge influx of vitamin via a wide range of different protective mechanisms. The mechanisms of uptake are slowed down, and the processes of metabolism and excretion are intensified. If taken in mega-doses, the water-soluble vitamins such as the B vitamins and vitamin C are excreted by the fastest possible route – into the urine – without being take up by the metabolism.

In the case of the fat-soluble vitamins A, D and E, mega-doses taken over long periods can endanger health. This is because these vitamins are not necessarily excreted, but are stored by the body. The symptoms of overdosage are usually similar to those of deficiency and, like the latter, may be life-threatening in their severity. In principle, megadoses of up to 100 times the recommended allowance should be taken only on prescription from a doctor; dosages like this are for specific curative purposes – for example, when treating severe nervous disorders.

Therapeutic agent for curing specific diseases

Vitamins as radical scavengers

Even though the recommended allowances for vitamins are now carefully calculated, we could still be getting too little of one particular type of vitamin. These are the antioxidant vitamins, of which there are three: beta-carotene (provitamin A), vitamin C and vitamin E. Antioxidant simply means that these vitamins occur in our metabolism as oxygen antagonists – in precisely those situations in which oxygen exhibits its less familiar, negative side rather than its good, beneficial characteristics.

Protection against Western diseases

In recent years, vitamin research has demonstrated more and more clearly that this antioxidant property could be used as a potential weapon against many diseases found in the Western world, for example, cancer, arteriosclerosis and myocardial infarction.

The action of antioxidants is based on their ability to render free radicals harmless. Before we can explain what this means, we must first take a close look at the role of oxygen in our metabolism.

Oxygen, with which every cell of the body is continuously supplied from the air we breathe, is required by the metabolism for the production of energy from nutrients. But unfortunately, oxygen also has a negative side: slowly but surely, it causes ageing. In the body it is responsible for the formation of free radicals. These are aggressive, oxygen-containing molecules with destructive activity which allow our cells and tissues to age. If our immune system is impaired, these molecules are free to exert their pathological activity. Although they lose their aggressive character in the process, they also cause severe damage to cells and tissues.

Oxygen enables radicals to form

Our cells are exposed to constant bombardment by free radicals, the formation of which is an unfortunate but inevitable secondary effect of a series of metabolic processes. The body has developed effective mechanisms in order to protect itself from the effects of these radicals. However, free radicals also attack from outside the body. A smoker inhales a few billion free radicals with every drag on a cigarette! UV radiation, air pollution and certain drugs similarly increase the formation of free radicals.

An internal
and external
threat

Free radicals are formed in the metabolism:	Free radicals are exogenous attackers:
• during energy production;	• due to environmental pollutants;
• through the activity of certain enzymes;	• due to cigarette smoke;
• in the immune system, where they help destroy invaders.	• due to UV and other radiation;
	• via the food we eat.

Notwithstanding the many mechanisms which protect against them, free radicals hit home again and again, causing damage to cell walls, cellular constituents, and even to the cell nuclei. These processes play an essential role in cellular ageing, ultimately contributing to ageing of the body as a whole. If the free radicals come into contact with the genetic material in the cell nucleus, a cellular transformation may take place and a cancer cell is formed. With their destructive action, radicals also appear to play a crucial role in the development of arteriosclerosis, certain types of rheumatism, and mental deterioration.

Destructive action

Free radicals increase the likelihood of many diseases	
• Cancer	• Arteriosclerosis
• Cataracts	• Skin diseases
• Certain forms of rheumatism and arthritis	• Alzheimer's disease (senile dementia)
• Parkinson's disease	• Radiation damage

How do antioxidants protect us?

By their ability to bind oxygen, the three antioxidants, vitamins C and E, and beta-carotene, act just like radical scavengers, thereby supporting the endogenous protective mechanisms of the body.

While we can do little to influence the body's own resistance to radicals, our intake of vitamins C and E and beta-carotene can easily be increased by selecting the right foods, or even by taking vitamin preparations. In this way we can build up special protection in stressful situations. It is not sufficient to get a good supply of only one of the three vitamins, for each one scavenges different types of radicals; only in combination do they constitute a truly wide-ranging front-line defence. Although final proof has yet to be presented, more and more researchers are of the opinion that a good antioxidant intake can help protect us from cancer, arteriosclerosis and heart attacks.

Decrease in the risk of disease

Strength through combined action

Vitamins in the fight against free radicals:
• Beta-carotene appears to considerably reduce the risk of lung cancer and cancers of the stomach and uterus. Smokers in particular should therefore pay special attention to ensuring a good intake of beta-carotene.
• Vitamins C and E are believed to be similar in their protective effect against the occurrence of cancer of the gastrointestinal tract, vitamin C being especially beneficial in protecting against cancers of the mouth, pharynx, oesophagus and pancreas.
• By protecting against free radicals, vitamins C and E prevent the formation of highly carcinogenic nitrosamines in the stomach. Nitrosamines are produced, for example, from nitrates in vegetables, or as a result of the grilling or roasting of cured meat containing nitrites.

The agent responsible for the deposits which clog the arteries of people with arteriosclerosis is a particular type of cholesterol, primarily oxidised cholesterol. Free radicals are also to blame for the oxidation process responsible for the production of this substance. Vitamins C and E act here too, as we have already seen: they protect cholesterol from oxidation, thus preventing, or slowing, the process of vascular sclerosis.

A number of studies now confirm that people with high blood levels of vitamins C and E develop arteriosclerosis and myocardial infarction more rarely than do those who receive insufficient of these vitamins. Vitamin C also appears to have a positive influence on hypertension.

During a study spanning several weeks in women suffering from hypertension a distinct reduction in the blood pressure was achieved with a daily dose of 1g vitamin C.

Free radicals are a contributory factor in certain forms of rheumatism and arthroses, and in Parkinson's disease. In studies of patients with rheumatic disorders the administration of high-dose vitamin E preparations led to alleviation of the symptoms in many cases.

There is also evidence that Alzheimer's disease, in which affected people suffer mental deterioration, is a consequence of free radicals attacking certain proteins in the brain. Research has yet to be done to ascertain whether antioxidants could be effective in this case.

Although these results are very promising, one thing must be remembered: while it is extremely likely that antioxidants help prevent cancer and other Western diseases, they cannot cure them! A diet rich in fruit, vegetables, nuts and vegetable oils ensures a high intake of beta-carotene, vitamin C and vitamin E. However, many experts believe that, in order to be certain of achieving the protective effect, your intake should be 5-10 times the RNI; this is possible only if a vitamin supplement is taken.

Vitamins at a glance

	Important for	Good sources	Signs of deficiency
Vitamin A (Beta-carotene)	Skin, hair, eyes, mucous membranes, cellular protection, growth and bone development	Green and yellow vegetables, liver, milk, butter, cheese *RNI* 1mg in 90g carrots 10g liver*	Scaly, dry skin, night-blindness, growth disorders, susceptibility to infection
Vitamin D	Osteogenesis (Prevention of-cancer?)	Fish, meat, fungi, eggs *RNI* 5µg in 20g of herrings*	Rickets, decalcification of bone
Vitamin E	Protects cells from radicals and oxidation	Vegetable oils and fats, e.g. wheat-germ oil and sunflower oil, nuts, avocados, peas *RNI* 12mg in 1 dessertspoonful of wheat-germ oil*	Myasthenia, anaemia, nervous disorders
Vitamin K	Coagulation of blood	Green vegetables, liver, eggs, milk, tomatoes *RNI* 65µg in 100g sauerkraut*	Increased tendency to haemorrhage
Vitamin B1 (thiamin)	Nerves, heart, muscles, carbohydrate metabolism	Wholemeal bread, potatoes, pulses pork, poultry *RNI* 1.2mg in 250g rolled oats*	Reduced ability to perform, nervous-ness, headache, cardiac disorders, convulsions, paralysis
Vitamin B2	Utilization of fat, protein and carbohydrates, growth	Milk, cheese, poultry, meat, cereals, yeast, fish *RNI* 1.6mg in 1L of milk*	Growth disorders, chapped lips and cracks at corners of mouth, disturbances of vision
Vitamin B6	Nerves, protein-metabolism, haematopoiesis	Fish, meat, wholemeal products, potatoes, soya *RNI* 1.6mg in 400g bananas*	Nausea, loss of appetite, muscular wasting, anaemia

*RNI = Reference Nutrient Intake for adults (as advised by the Manual of Nutrition - MAFF Reference book 342 10th edition, HMSO 1985 1µg (microgram) = 0.001mg (milligram)

	Important for	Good sources	Signs of deficiency
Vitamin B12	Haematopoiesis, cell structure, growth	Liver, herring, beef, eggs, milk, quark *RNI* 5µg in 150g Camembert*	Anaemia, tiredness, nervous disorders
Niacin	Heart, nerves, central nervous system, metabolism	Wholemeal bread, peas, meat, salt-water fish, salmon, fungi *RNI* 16.5mg in 150g chicken breast*	Tiredness, depression, nervous disorders, pellagra
Pantothenic acid	Catabolism of fats, carbohy-drates and proteins, hormone production, skin and mucosae	Liver, broccoli, cauliflower, veal and beef, turkey, milk, fungi, saltwater fish, poultry *RNI* 6mg in 300g mushrooms*	Skin damage, susceptibility to infections, nervous disorders
Folic acid	Haematopoiesis, cell division	Green vegetables, cabbage, pulses, liver, wholemeal produce, potatoes *RNI* 300µg in 300g broccoli*	Anaemia, digestive disorders, mucosa alterations
Biotin	Skin and hair; carbohydrate and fatty-acid anabolism	Milk, liver, pulses, mushrooms, spinach *RNI* 100µg in-100g liver*	Hair loss, skin changes, nausea
Vitamin C	Immune response, formation of connective tissue and bone, use of iron, haemato-poiesis	Citrus fruits, paprika, kiwis, cauliflower, tomatoes, *RNI* 75mg in 1 kiwi or 2 large oranges*	Susceptibility to infection, decreased performance, scurvy

Vitamin A

Vitamin D

Vitamin E

The fat-soluble vitamins

The fat-soluble vitamins A, D, E and K are taken up and
digested by the body together with, or as fats.
With the exception of vitamin K, the body is capable of
storing these vitamins in varying degrees. These reserves
can in some cases safeguard our supply for a matter of
months, even if little or none of these vitamins are ingested
in the diet during this time.

Vitamin K

Vitamin A – the all-rounder

So much has recently been said and written about vitamin A that it could soon replace vitamin C as the most popular of the vitamins. Vitamin A has long been known to be important for the eyes and skin, and for growth. Now the results of vitamin research confirm that it also fulfils important functions as a radical scavenger, and thus has a preventive action against certain types of cancer and cardiovascular disease.

Crystals of pure vitamin A

Beta-carotene

In the developing world, millions of people still suffer from acute vitamin A deficiency. Children are worst affected. According to estimates of the World Health Organization (WHO), every year half a million children throughout the world go blind as a result of vitamin A deficiency; two-thirds of the children die within a few weeks of going blind.

Why we need vitamin A
Vitamin A intervenes in many different metabolic processes of the body. Here are the most important areas in which it is needed and is beneficial:
• The skin. Vitamin A is essential for healthy skin and the functioning of the mucous membranes. The mucous membranes of the nose, throat, intestine, bladder, lungs and eyes all depend on vitamin A in just the same way as the skin.

• Sexuality and reproduction. Vitamin A is required for sexual and reproductive function. It is involved in the production of the male sex hormone testosterone and without vitamin A a male cannot produce sperm. A female cannot conceive without vitamin A because it is essential for the formation of the placenta and the development of the embryo.

For correct vision

• The eyes. We need vitamin A to enable us to see. With the aid of retinol (vitamin A1), the eye synthesizes rhodopsin, often known as visual purple. This substance enables us to see in the dark, and to see colours.

• Bones and the skeletal system. Vitamin A is needed for the development of the bones and skeleton.

• Protection from cancer and cardiovascular disease. Whereas many of the changes which occur in the skin as a result of vitamin A deficiency (for example, keratinization of skin and mucosae) are the same as the preliminary stages of cancer, many studies have now revealed that individuals who have a poor vitamin A intake have a higher incidence of cancer than those whose vitamin A intake is good. This appears to be linked first and foremost to the activity of beta-carotene as a radical scavenger and antioxidant, which is believed also to be responsible for the possible protective action of carotenoids against cardiovascular disease.

Strengthens the immune system

• Protection against infection. Vitamin A also fulfils important functions within the immune system. Deficiency considerably increases the susceptibility of the body to infectious diseases.

Deficiency: the eyes and skin suffer first

Anyone who suddenly experiences difficulty seeing in twilight conditions or in the dark should also consider the possibility of vitamin A deficiency.

Skin and hair also suffer

Night-blindness is one of the first signs of severe vitamin A deficiency. Skin and hair also suffer when stored vitamin A begins to decline. The skin becomes scaly, cracked and dry and begins to keratinize, and the hair loses its lustre and begins to break easily, as do the fingernails.

Severe vitamin A deficiency is associated with the

clinical picture of xerophthalmia, in which night-blindness develops into total blindness. Infective agents colonise damaged skin and mucosae, and affected mucosae of the bronchi and lungs lose their resistance; often a pulmonary infection occurs, with fatal outcome. In developing countries, vitamin A deficiency is the most important vitamin deficiency state.

Infections of skin and mucosae

Even natural healers in the past knew, as they did in many other cases too, what substance should be used to treat disorders caused by a lack of vitamin A, without knowing anything about the actual chemical structure of the vitamin. As long as 3,500 years ago, the Egyptian physicians of the day used to treat patients suffering from night-blindness with oil obtained from the livers of fish caught in the river Nile. Around 400 years B.C., Hippocrates was treating similarly afflicted patients with raw ox-liver dipped in honey. Nowadays, we know through research that liver can indeed be one of the major sources of vitamin A in our diet.

The major sources of vitamin A

True vitamin A, chemical name retinol, is found only in animal produce. Apart from liver, the principal sources of especially large amounts of vitamin A are butter, high-fat cheeses, whole milk, poultry, and oily fish such as tuna, herring, mackerel and canned sardines. As a fat-soluble vitamin, vitamin A usually occurs in abundance in particularly fatty foods.

Retinol occurs only in animal produce

Just as important as retinol are its precursors, the provitamins, which occur exclusively in vegetable produce and are converted into retinol in the intestinal wall. The most important provitamin A is beta-carotene; the name 'carotene' is derived from 'carrot', and was given to this particular provitamin A because it is present in carrots in high concentration. Many yellow-green vegetables, such as endives, broccoli, chicory, spinach and lettuce are also important providers of carotene. Of the fruits and berries, apricots, elderberries and mangos are especially good sources of carotene.

Beta-carotene in fruit and vegetables

• As large as possible a proportion of the vitamin A requirement should be obtained as beta-carotene from fruit and vegetables, for only beta-carotene has the described action as an antioxidant and radical scavenger, possibly protecting against cancer and arteriosclerosis.

Requirement and high-risk groups

Retinol equivalent units

In dietary recommendations and in food tables, the vitamin A requirement and the vitamin A content of foods are usually given in what are called 'retinol-equivalent' units. These give a unit of measurement which encompasses both true vitamin A, retinol, and the carotenoids as provitamins.

The basic underlying assumption here is that on average our metabolism converts the beta-carotene ingested with food into about 17% as much usable retinol. This conversion is already incorporated in retinol-equivalent units. Thus the retinol-equivalent content in 100g of carrots indicates the amount of active retinol the body on average produces from the carotene content of this weight of carrots.

The vitamin A requirement is normally achieved through a normal varied diet. However, there are some groups who have an increased requirement, or whose intake is at risk; particular factors also make it necessary to increase the intake of the vitamin:

Groups at risk

• Pregnant women need about 30% more vitamin A than average, and breast-feeding women about 100% more.
• Young women may, as a result of frequent crash dieting, find themselves in a state of undernourishment and malnutrition which may also result in an imbalance of the vitamin A intake.
• Elderly people often have a poor vitamin A or beta-carotene intake owing to a poor, or unbalanced diet.
• Chronic disorders of fat digestion, Crohn's disease, insulin-dependent diabetes, diseases of the pancreas, and alcoholism can trigger vitamin A deficiency which, in some circumstances, necessitates treatment with vitamin A supplements.

Vitamin A in the daily diet

Only 10% of the beta-carotene in carrots – which are particularly rich in the provitamin – is absorbed from raw carrots. However, we now know that the carotene uptake from vegetables and fruit can be greatly increased in the following ways:

How to optimize your vitamin A intake

• The more finely the vegetable is chopped, the more carotene is absorbed from it. We can therefore boost our carotene intake by grating, sieving or puréeing carotene-containing vegetables.

• Always prepare carotene-containing vegetables with a little fat, for example by adding a knob of butter during steaming, or by mixing a little oil with raw salad. Fat helps improve the bioavailability of carotene quite considerably. It has also been shown that saturated fatty acids, which are found primarily in animal fats, achieve a better transportation effect than unsaturated ones.

• By satisfying your vitamin A requirement with beta-carotene from fruit and vegetables, you are immediately achieving two things at once: firstly, there is no risk of overdosage, because excess vitamin is excreted by the kidneys, in contrast to vitamin A from animal produce which is stored in the liver; secondly, in eating vegetable food produce you are as a rule absorbing especially large amounts of other important vitamins, minerals and roughage.

Beware of too much vitamin A

Anyone who takes high-dose vitamin A supplements over long periods in addition to their normal diet is at risk of hypervitaminosis – overdosage sufficiently high as to be harmful. Even a natural intake from the diet can result in hypervitaminosis. While polar-bear liver would admittedly be an unusually exotic delicacy, it is the richest of all food sources of vitamin A. The 60 or so milligrams of vitamin A per gram present in polar-bear liver is certainly enough to induce vitamin A poisoning, with headache, dizziness and vomiting. Even for the Eskimos, who enjoy the occasional piece of polar-bear meat, the polar-bear liver is taboo.

Too much can be dangerous

Patients who had ingested about 12 times the recommended allowance of vitamin A every day for two years suffered skin changes, hair loss, pains in the bones and joints, muscle stiffness and enlargement of the liver; women additionally experienced amenorrhoea. Once the vitamin A intake was discontinued, the symptoms disappeared within only a few weeks.

Symptoms of overdosage

Recommended daily allowance in adults: 0.8–1.0mg

How much vitamin A does our food contain?

Quantity	Food	Content mg	% of RNI	
150g	Spinach, raw	1.2		133%
150g	Carrots, raw	1.7		188%
200g	Leeks, raw	0.66	73%	
20	Lamb's liver	1.2		133%
25g	Liver sausage, lean	0.38	42%	
150g	Mackerel	1.47		163%
30g	Camembert, 45% fat	0.15	16%	
25g	Butter	0.16	17%	
20g	Egg yolk	0.3	33%	

Uses of vitamin A in medicine

Vitamin A preparations can be used to treat a whole range of illnesses:
• A susceptibility to inflammation of the mucous membranes, especially those of the respiratory tract which can lead to bronchitis, influenza infections and laryngitis.
• Dryness of the skin causing scaling, keratinization, desquamation, skin impurities and even acne can all be treated successfully with vitamin A.
• Vitamin A is helpful in a whole range of eye disorders, for example hypersensitivity to light or drying of the cornea and conjunctivae.
• Always consult your doctor before taking high-dose vitamin A preparations.

Prescribed by the doctor

Vitamin D – a renewable source

Strictly speaking, vitamin D is not a vitamin at all, for unlike all the other vitamins it can be produced in the body. However, to do this the body needs the assistance of an external energy source: the sun. Without this, or rather without its UV radiation, the provitamin which is deposited in the skin cannot be converted into the active form.

Provitamin D3 is manufactured from cholesterol by the liver. From the liver it passes through the bloodstream to the skin, where it remains until activated by radiation. Two

ten-minute sunbathing sessions a week are all that is required to provide the body with an adequate quantity of cholecalciferol, the chemical name for vitamin D3. Provided that there is enough sun, vitamin D becomes a self-renewing source from which the body can supply itself without an intake from food.

Illustration shows Vitamin D

Vitamin D strengthens the bones

The body needs two minerals, calcium and phosphate, for a healthy skeleton and bone renewal. But, even if the two minerals are available in optimum quantity, healthy bone development is only achieved in the presence of adequate vitamin D. This is because vitamin D promotes the absorption of calcium and phosphate from the intestine and controls the incorporation of calcium and phosphorus in the bones.

Conversely, it can also cause calcium and phosphorus to be released from the bones, and in the kidneys it ensures that no more calcium is excreted than is necessary. In short, without vitamin D there can be no controlled balance of calcium and phosphate and thus no problem-free anabolism of bone. Vitamin D also influences the process of cell division, and could therefore play a role in the occurrence of cancer or its prevention. In one scientific study in which breast-cancer surgery and irradiation were followed by treatment with vitamin D, 70% of the women remained healthy for long periods, whereas 60% of the women in the group which did not receive vitamin D suffered recurrence of the cancer.

Psoriasis, too, can in many cases be alleviated by internal or external treatment with vitamin D tablets or vitamin D cream. However, the use of vitamin D will not lead to a complete cure.

Positive influence on cancer and psoriasis

Deficiency: Rickets is very rare these days

If vitamin D had already been discovered at the time the hunchback of Notre-Dame was published, the story would never have been written. For centuries, rickets crippled countless people during childhood, and there was no known cure.

Today our knowledge of rickets is based almost exclusively on historical data, although isolated cases of rickets have recently occurred again as a result of mothers, for ideological reasons, or as part of an 'alternative' dietary regimen, withholding from their young children the requisite preventive measure in the form of their daily vitamin D supplement.

Severe rickets causes malformation of the sternum, the bones of the skull and the spinal column, and often the jaw is deformed, while the bones break if subjected to the slightest load. In adults, rickets causes osteomalacia, or softening of the bones.

Irreparable damage

The most important sources of vitamin D

Babies are at particular risk of impaired vitamin D intake, as they are kept indoors for much of the time. Before vitamin D supplements became available, cod-liver oil was one of the few vitamin foods known to be rich in vitamin D. So a generation of children were subjected to daily doses of cod-liver oil which were poured down their throats regardless of its terrible taste.

Otherwise, vitamin D is present in very few foods in appreciable concentrations: salt-water fish – especially salmon, mackerel, herring, sardines, tuna and halibut – fungi, egg yolk and butter are the most important ones.

Requirement and high-risk groups

The lack of foods containing vitamin D means that achieving the recommended amount from our daily diet is no easy matter. However, the situation has been improved in that the majority of margarines and infant foods are now enriched with vitamin D.

• Neither breast milk nor cows' milk contain an adequate quantity of vitamin D, so it is very important to ensure that babies get their daily vitamin D supplement. Premature babies have a particularly high requirement for the vitamin.

• Strict vegetarians and vegans are also at risk. Individuals who eat no animal fats receive only minimal amounts of the vegetable provitamin from their diet. This can increase the risk of postmenopausal osteoporosis, particularly in women who are strict vegetarians.

• Heavy smokers often have a drastically reduced vitamin D level so they, too, need to make sure that they have a higher than average intake of vitamin D.

• Immigrants to the UK from countries further south are also in a high-risk group. In countries where the sun shines almost every day, the metabolism operates on a genetically-controlled economy program of vitamin production in the skin. Because of our climate 'immigrant osteomalacia' has now become quite common in this country amongst the immigrant population.

• Elderly people are often found to have a low vitamin D level. In many cases they spend too little time out in the sun; this problem is further compounded by the fact that vitamin D synthesis in the skin declines continuously as we get older.

• Although protection against sunlight or UV radiation is essential, as always, too much of a good thing can be harmful. Powerful UV sun blockers prevent sunburn but they also prevent the formation of vitamin D in the skin.

• An excess of vitamin D may also be damaging. Although there is very little possibility of vitamin D intoxication from the food we eat, and the skin protects itself from too much sun with increased pigmentation thereby simultaneously limiting vitamin D production, anyone taking vitamin D preparations is likely to be at risk from overdose unless they take adequate precautions. Even ten times the recommended daily amount can be damaging in the long term. Loss of appetite, nausea, vomiting and headache are the first symptoms. Excess vitamin D mobilises calcium from the bones, which become brittle as a result. The liberated calcium may in turn lead to calcifications in the kidneys.

Symptoms of overdosage

• Vitamin D supplements should only be used following consultation with a doctor.

Recommended daily allowance in adults: 5µg

Quantity	Food	Content µg		% of RNI	
50g	White fish	3.45		69%	
20g	Salmon	3.26			65.2%
150g	Chicken liver	1.19	23.8%		
150g	Mushrooms	2.7		54%	
100g	Egg yolk	2.0	40%		

How much vitamin D does our food contain?

Uses of vitamin D in medicine

The dose for rickets prophylaxis in babies and small children is 12.5-25µg vitamin D per day. In adults, vitamin D is used prophylactically against osteomalacia(softening of the bones) and as an adjuvant measure in the treatment of osteoporosis (demineralization of bone).

The vitamin for healthy bone

Vitamin E – the wonder drug?

Vitamin E first made its name as a fertility drug. In 1922, the American scientists Evans, Scott and Bishop discovered that rats fed a diet of milk protein, maize starch, dripping and butter developed severe fertility problems, which led to

complete infertility in the second generation. But when the scientists fed them wheat-germ and a little hay, they suddenly began to produce live young again.

The unknown fertility factor was identified by Evans a short time later in the wheat-germ, and he called it Tocopherol, which means 'aiding birth', – vitamin E had been

Illustration shows vitamin E

discovered. Unfortunately, hopes that taking this substance would solve all our infertility problems remained unfulfilled. Although vitamin E deficiency does cause infertility in humans, there are many other factors which play a role in sexual dysfunction.

Perhaps our recent expectations of this vitamin are simply too high. Vitamin E is today considered as a potential weapon against myocardial infarction, cancer, rheumatism and ageing of the skin, but we should also bear in mind that its preventive action is principally attributable to its property as a radical scavenger.

Vitamin E protects cells from free radicals

Protection of cells from free radicals

Protection of the body from free radicals and antioxidant activity are now regarded as the most important functions of vitamin E. By its antioxidant properties, it prevents peroxidation of unsaturated fats in the tissues, while at the same time protecting cell walls, cell membranes and hormones. This protection naturally extends to the cells in the walls of our blood vessels – this is where the preventive action of vitamin E against arteriosclerosis begins.

Vitamin E inactivates oxygen radicals which may be formed as a result of environmental toxins or smoking, but are also due to endogenous processes of the body, and which prepare the way for cellular ageing and cancer. Studies have shown that a low level of vitamin E in the blood increases the likelihood of cancer.

Vitamin E is also believed to have a protective effect on the skin; many cosmetic treatment preparations and many anti-sun creams already contain vitamin E. With these products we are promised protection from the radicals which can be formed in the skin as a result of intensive UV irradiation. Vitamin E is believed to regenerate and smooth the skin, and to increase its moisture retention capacity.

Nurtures and protects skin and tissue

• Vitamin E keeps the blood flowing. It regulates the blood clotting, at the same time ensuring good blood flow; it is also able to dilate constricted blood vessels.

• Vitamin E improves the supply and utilization of oxygen in the tissue thus protecting, among other things, the liver, lungs and skin from inflammation and degenerative processes.

Vitamin E also has quite a range of other functions, which have still not been researched in detail. For example, it appears to play equally significant roles in manufacturing the protein of the body, in energy transport within the cells, and in the dissemination of genetic information.

There is no typical deficiency disease

The inability of scientists to agree on clearly defined requirements for vitamin E intake is in part linked to the fact that deficiency phenomena are very difficult to identify. There are none of the typical deficiency diseases which exist for other vitamins, yet a low vitamin E level is regularly identified as a secondary sign of many diseases, for example in patients with myocardial infarction or cancer. External symptoms such as myasthenia, impaired reflexes, disturbances of vision, facial cramps, and even tiredness and an inability to concentrate may be consequences of a poor vitamin E intake.

Symptoms of deficiencies

Sources and availability

Vegetable fats and oils such as margarine, olive oil, sunflower oil and soya-bean oil, among many others, are extremely rich sources of vitamin E. Nuts, grain, and various vegetables such as spinach, celery and broccoli are also rich in vitamin E.

Vegetable fats and oils

Recommended daily allowance in adults: 12mg

How much vitamin E does our food contain?

Quantity	Food	Content mg	% of RNI	
20g	Olive oil	2.7	22.5%	
10g	Wheat-germ oil	15.9		132.5 %
20g	Margarine	2.7	22,5%	
150g	Norwegian red fish	1.95	16%	
150g	Turkey	2.85	24%	
20g	Hazelnuts	4.2	35%	
20g	Sunflower kernels	4.36	36%	
150g	Asparagus, raw	3.15	26%	
200g	Peas, raw	6.0	50%	
150g	Avocado, raw	4.5	37.5%	

Requirement and high-risk groups

Based on the body's requirement it seems more or less certain that we get sufficient vitamin E from food as the requirement of 12mg per day should be easily achieved from our daily diet.

Pregnant and breast-feeding women have an increased requirement, as do people suffering from stress, and those whose diet includes a high proportion of unsaturated fatty acids, present mainly in vegetable fats and oils. Under conditions of stress the body's systems are exposed to more pronounced oxidation processes; the body must therefore be protected with supplementary vitamin E. In the case of unsaturated fatty acids, the starting assumption is that for each additional gram in the diet, 0.5mg of supplementary vitamin E is required. However, since it is precisely the vegetable fats and oils which contain especially large amounts of vitamin E, as a rule the recommended increased requirement is usually well covered by the vitamin content.

Pregnant women and people suffering from stress

Is the recommended amount enough?

In response to the findings from research reports, that vitamin E can protect from cancer and arteriosclerosis, some experts are already advocating 5-10 times the recommended amount. Even with a regular vitamin E intake of 300mg per day, corresponding to 25 times the daily recommendation, no signs of damage or intoxication phenomena arise. Caution is, however, necessary at dosages of 400mg and more per day. In a study involving chronic administration of 800mg per day, myasthenia and exhaustion were the first signs of hypervitaminosis.

Vitamin K – prevents a simple scratch from being fatal

Daily life is full of minor risks, for who hasn't suffered the occasional cut, puncture wound or knock and lost a little blood? That a minor trauma like this does not prove fatal is thanks to vitamin K, for without this vitamin we would inevitably bleed to death from the smallest wound.

Vitamin K coagulates the blood

In order for blood clotting to occur, a whole series of coagulation factors must come into play. If even a single one of these factors is lost, the system is critically disturbed and bleeding continues. Some of these coagulation factors cannot be produced without the assistance of vitamin K.

Illustration shows vitamin K

Vitamin K deficiency

In healthy adults, vitamin K deficiency is almost non-existent owing to the extensive availability of the vitamin in our diet.

However, deficiency phenomena may still arise, for example if the intestinal flora are destroyed by antibiotic therapy, if the

absorption of vitamin K from the diet is impaired due to disturbance of fat digestion, or when patients, for example those with a tendency to thrombosis, receive long-term treatment with anticoagulant drugs.

Nosebleeds, heavy periods, wounds which heal badly because they do not form a scab, are the external signs of deficiency. Internal signs may be spontaneous gastrointestinal haemorrhaging, haemorrhaging from mucosae, in the lungs, liver or brain, and on the retina of the eye.

Symptoms of deficiency

Where vitamin K is found

Vitamin K1 is present in many vegetables, and is especially abundant in green leafy vegetables. Vitamin K2 is produced by bacteria, and is also a constituent of many animal products such as meat, milk, cheese and butter.

Even the bacteria in the flora of the human large intestine are enthusiastic producers of vitamin K. The body is able to absorb small quantities of this bacterial vitamin, thus ensuring a minimum intake.

Vitamin K courtesy of the intestinal flora

Requirement and high-risk groups

Before birth, a baby's vitamin K supply is extremely poor; this is because only traces of the vitamin pass through the placenta. The neonatal intestine is still sterile, and lacks the bacteria necessary for endogenous production of vitamin K.

Breast milk contains relatively little vitamin K, and during the first few days of life wholly breast-fed newborns are exposed to a rare, but potentially dangerous form of brain haemorrhage. In severe cases, the bleeding can be life-threatening. Haemorrhaging of this type can be successfully treated with vitamin K in the form of a pharmaceutical product which is given as an injection or drops.

Newborn babies do not get enough vitamin K

However, doubts are now being raised as to the safety of this procedure. According to the results of a recent study, injections of vitamin K given immediately after birth could predispose to leukaemia. However, it should be noted that these results are only speculative and can in no way be regarded as confirmed.

The pros and cons of vitamin K injections

Recommended daily allowance in adults: 60-80µg

Quantity	Food	Content µg	% of RNI
25g	Roast chicken	75	107%
30g	Roast beef	45	64%
50g	Soya beans	90	129%
20g	Green peas, raw	60	86%
15g	Cauli, spinach, raw	450	643%
10g	Broccoli, tomato, raw	80	114%

Use of vitamin K in medicine

The most important application relates to vitamin K deficiency-induced haemorrhage. Patients at risk of thrombosis are frequently treated with drugs which inhibit blood clotting. Vitamin K ampoules are available for these patients; they should carry the ampoules with them at all times, so that if they ever injure themselves they can restore normal blood clotting as quickly as possible.

Vitamin B2

Vitamin B6

Biotin

Vitamin B12

Pantothenic
acid

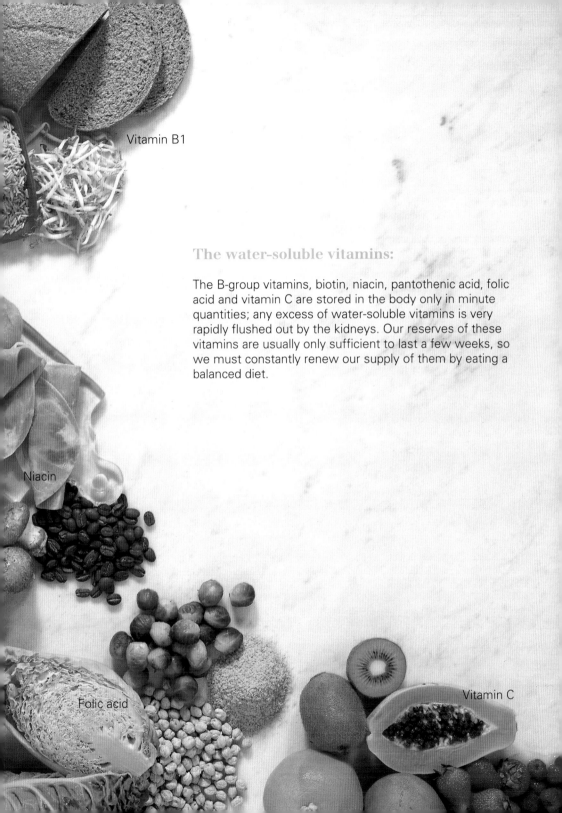

Vitamin B1

Niacin

Folic acid

Vitamin C

The water-soluble vitamins:

The B-group vitamins, biotin, niacin, pantothenic acid, folic acid and vitamin C are stored in the body only in minute quantities; any excess of water-soluble vitamins is very rapidly flushed out by the kidneys. Our reserves of these vitamins are usually only sufficient to last a few weeks, so we must constantly renew our supply of them by eating a balanced diet.

Vitamin B1 – provides energy and strengthens the nerves

Vitamin B1, also called thiamine, is probably the most familiar of the eight B-group vitamins. Perhaps this is because, among other reasons, the vitamin B1 intake of many people is still relatively poor. Vitamin B1 is often referred to as the 'nerve vitamin', as the nervous system is one of the most important areas in which vitamin B1 expresses its activity; moreover, it is here that the first symptoms of vitamin B1 deficiency occur, at first in systemic signs such as a lack of concentration and tiredness.

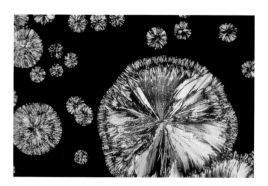

Illustration shows vitamin B1

Vitamin B1 maintains the flow of energy
Without thiamine, carbohydrates such as sugar or starch cannot be broken down into smaller molecules. If this situation does occur it is likely to have fatal consequences. It is vital that all carbohydrates in the body are converted into glucose because this is the crucial supplier of energy to the cells. If the conversion of glucose to energy ceases, this will ultimately mean that the energy flow is interrupted.

Whereas the majority of cells in the body have some recourse to other substances for their energy supply, the brain depends exclusively on glucose for its energy.

However, this is not the only reason for calling vitamin B1 the 'nerve vitamin': it is also thought to have other functions in the nervous system, for which there are a series of indicators. Although these have not yet been clarified they are thought to have an important part to play within the nervous system.

• Without thiamine energy flow ceases.

Symptoms
affect the
circulation

First signs of vitamin B1 deficiency

The first symptoms resemble mild disturbances of the circulation: they begin with tingling in the arms and legs, and a sensation of the feet having 'gone to sleep' is also a common occurrence. In later stages the muscles of the legs become weaker, and paralysis may eventually occur as the joints stiffen and the nerves become inflamed. These symptoms may be accompanied by psychological problems and convulsions and eventually death may result from cardiovascular failure.

Right up until the twentieth century countless people, mainly inhabitants of the countries of south-east Asia, died of beriberi, the classical thiamine deficiency disease. Their staple diet was milled rice, which contains no thiamine as all the vitamin B1 present in rice is in the husk. Even today many people, mainly Asians, become ill with thiamine deficiency disease due to malnutrition. Although beriberi is unknown in countries with a high standard of living, mild forms of vitamin B1 deficiency can occur here too. Essentially, this deficiency manifests itself as two types of symptoms:
• Disturbances of the cardiovascular system, such as breathing difficulties, tightness of the chest, cardiac pain, and palpitations.
• Neurological disturbances and psychological problems such as tiredness, lack of concentration, impaired attentiveness, irritability, depression and anxiety.

Sources and availability

Although vitamin B1 is present in almost all foods, this does not mean that a good intake can be taken for granted, for many foods contain only traces of the vitamin. The most important suppliers of thiamine are wholemeal products and pork; with regard to vegetables, peas are particularly rich in thiamine. Thanks to a general trend away from white flours, which are low in nutrients and roughage, and towards wholemeal flours, our thiamine intake has also improved. There are now white flours which still contain the wheat-germ, a particularly rich source of vitamin B1.

Only traces
are present
in many
foods

Requirement and high-risk groups

Owing to the particular role of thiamine in carbohydrate metabolism, people on a diet rich in carbohydrate have an increased vitamin B1 requirement. In general our daily requirement is considered to be 0.33mg of thiamine per 1,000kcal. Individuals whose energy consumption is distinctly higher than normal, for example people who take part in active sports, or those who do physically demanding work need more thiamine than average.

Thiamine is one of the vitamins with which many age groups and many sectors of the population are relatively poorly supplied, although this does not mean that we should interpret these as true deficiency states. But the very fact that values at the lower limit of the normal range are common is sufficient justification for taking care to ensure that our own intake is good. Some reasons for dietary deficiencies are as follows:

• Nutritional imbalances, for example those associated with long-term crash dieting and very strict dietary regimens.

• Age-related nutritional imbalances, one example is elderly people who no longer get enough variety in what they eat owing to food intolerances.

• Alcohol abuse, because alcohol impairs thiamine metabolism and increases the thiamine requirement.

• Diseases of the gastrointestinal tract, in which the absorption and utilization of thiamine is disturbed.

Recommended daily allowance in adults: 1.3–1.6mg

Quantity	Food	Content mg	% of RNI	
10g	Brewer's yeast	1.2		83%
150g	Pork, lean.	1.05		72%
150g	Chicken breast	0.75		52%
150g	Plaice	0.32	22%	
150g	Wholewheat bread	0.38	26%	
30g	Wheat-germ	0.6	41%	
250g	Potatoes	0.25	17%	
50g	Rice	0.2	14%	
150g	Peas	0.52	36%	

Thiamine – an ephemeral and sensitive vitamin

Water and heat destroy thiamine

Thiamine is a sensitive vitamin. For one thing, it leaches out easily when food products are washed. It is also highly sensitive to temperature, with the result that much of it is lost during the cooking process. Thiamine-rich foods should therefore be handled with the maximum possible care, and be heated for the shortest possible time at the lowest temperature possible. Even when simply toasting bread, 40-50% of the thiamine present is lost. A third of the vitamin B1 present in milk is destroyed during sterilization.

Apart from the sensitivity of vitamin B1, many foods contain agents which have a destructive action on this vitamin. Blackberries, blackcurrants, beetroot, brussel sprouts and red cabbage all contain thiaminase, a substance which destroys thiamine. If thiamine-rich foods are eaten together with foods containing thiaminase, the thiamine is destroyed before it can be absorbed. Raw fish also contains large quantities of thiaminase; this is often the reason why a poor thiamine intake is still a problem in Asia, where a lot of raw fish is eaten. Thiaminase in fish is destroyed by boiling or other heat treatment.

Thiaminase destroys vitamin

The absorption of thiamine from the diet is improved by eating thiamine-rich foods together with vegetable fats such as sunflower oil, which have a high content of unsaturated fatty acids, or with vitamin C-rich foods like fruit or vegetables.

As a water-soluble vitamin, the total quantity of thiamine present in the body is only about 25mg. For this reason alone, it is important to ensure that you are getting a regular intake, since deficiency can set in after only a few weeks. This explains why frequent crash dieting and fad diets rapidly lead to vitamin B1 deficiency.

Deficiency due to crash dieting

Thiamine is also a medicinal substance

Today, high-dose vitamin B1 is used in a great many neurological diseases. Good results with high-dose vitamin B1 have also been observed in pain therapy. Thiamine in tablet form has been used to alleviate pain in patients with headache, spinal syndrome, painful joints and neuralgia.

Few side-effects There is scarcely any risk of side-effects from the administration of very high doses of thiamine. In the very few cases in which reactions did occur following administration of extremely high doses – in excess of 500mg taken intravenously – the symptoms were sweating, breathing difficulty, palpitations and a sensation of heat.

Vitamin B2 – starts the metabolism going

Vitamin B2, which is also called riboflavin, is rather an inconspicuous vitamin. So far, at any rate, it has failed to acquire a name for itself as a potential miracle cure for any disease prevalent in the West. In our metabolism, however, it plays a very important role. Without vitamin B2, literally nothing would work; for like thiamine, this vitamin is involved at the centre of energy production.

Riboflavin converts food into energy

When we talk about burning nutrients – carbohydrates, fats and proteins – we are describing the fact that all usable food ultimately serves the body for energy production. To this end, the nutrients are broken down to the simplest anabolic components in complex cycles such as glycolysis and ß-oxidation. This process, which takes place in all cells, is also known as the respiratory chain. The fact that riboflavin is used in the respiratory chain means that every cell of the body needs vitamin B2 to live.

Illustration shows vitamin B2

In addition to this central role in the context of energy production, riboflavin also fulfils other functions:
• It is involved in the production and destruction of red blood cells, it assists with the detoxification activities of the liver, and it plays an important role in the growth and development of the embryo.

54

• Vitamin B2 is also used in the metabolism of the eye. Riboflavin is thought to have a protective effect against the effects of light, and is necessary for night vision.
• In the nervous system it is concerned with maintenance of the myelin sheath, the protective layer surrounding the nerves.

Vitamin B2 is also believed to be required for a functioning immune system.

True deficiency is rare

Severe vitamin B2 deficiency is extremely rare. If it does occur, it is often associated with deficiency of other B-group vitamins or niacin, for example in pellagra, which arises from a combined under-supply of riboflavin and niacin.

The first indications of riboflavin deficiency may be tiredness and poor concentration. Inflammation of the oral mucosa and cracks at the corners of the mouth may also occur; the skin becomes flaky and red patches appear.

Sources and availability

Many foods contain vitamin B2. Particularly good sources are milk, cheese, meat, fish, eggs and wholemeal products. If you drink a lot of milk, you have no need to worry about your vitamin B2 intake. Half a litre a day will provide all you need. Increased consumption of milk and cheese, especially among young people, has led in recent years to a considerable improvement in our intake.

Requirement and high-risk groups

The recommended nutrient intake of riboflavin is 1.7mg per day for men, and 1.5mg for women. In pregnant and breast-feeding women, the requirement increases to 1.8mg and 2.3mg respectively. While it is true that, in adults, riboflavin doses as low as 0.8-0.9mg per day prevent deficiency phenomena, at this dosage the intake can only be regarded as inadequate.

Since vitamin B2 is also important for energy metabolism, the riboflavin intake must also be guided by energy consumption. Individuals on long-term diets should not allow their minimum daily intake of vitamin B2 to fall below 1.2mg, so as not to provoke metabolic disturbances. After all, even if we starve ourselves the basal metabolism (the amount of energy required to sustain life when at rest) must still be covered at all times. If there is any doubt about your intake, especially during periods of dieting, the vitamin B2 supply should be safeguarded by means of a vitamin supplement.

Adolescents between the ages of 15 and 18 years have a higher requirement: 1.8mg in males and 1.7mg in females. Deficiency or impaired intake is most frequently identified in this group. However, the incidence of impaired intake is above average among 18-35 year old women, weight-reducing diets are usually the most important cause of this deficit.

The intake must be safeguarded even when dieting

Chronic alcohol abuse, heavy smoking, the contraceptive pill and certain psychoactive drugs such as the 'tricyclic' antidepressants, digestive disorders and strict vegetarianism, or veganism, may be other causes of impaired vitamin B2 intake or a true vitamin B2 deficiency. Vegans do not eat any meat or milk, dairy products, fish or eggs because they are animal produce; this means that they are excluding the major sources of riboflavin from their diet.

• Yeast provides an excellent means of improving our riboflavin intake, as it is one of the richest of all sources of vitamin B2. However, yeast consumption should not become a long-term habit, as too much yeast increases the risk of gout.

Riboflavin is sensitive to light

Although riboflavin is fairly heat-resistant, this advantage is offset by its sensitivity to light. To give an example, in order to avoid high losses of vitamin B2, milk in clear-glass bottles should be exposed to daylight as little as possible.

There is no evidence that too much riboflavin is harmful. As with all other water-soluble vitamins, our metabolism has a tailor-made solution to megadoses of vitamin B2: the excess is excreted rapidly via the kidneys, staining the urine deep yellow. The intense yellow coloration is a typical characteristic of pure riboflavin, so no one who drinks a lot of milk or is taking a vitamin B preparation should be surprised if their urine is deep yellow.

Recommended daily allowance in adults: 1.5-1.7mg

How much
vitamin B2
does our food
contain?

Quantity	Food	Content mg	% of RNI	
50g	Pig's liver	1.6		100%
100g	Chicken breast	0.9	62%	
150g	Pollack, mackerel	0.53	37%	
20g	Brewer's yeast	0.75	47%	
150g	Spinach, broccoli, raw	0.3	19%	
150g	Yoghurt, 3.5% fat	0.27	16%	
500g	Long-life or fresh milk	0.9	62%	
30g	Wheat-germ	0.22	14%	

Vitamin B6 – regulates chemical changes in the body

In 1934 a vitamin researcher, Szent-Györgyi, fed young rats a synthetic feed supplemented with vitamins B1 and B2 and the animals very soon became severely damaged; the fur on their heads and paws fell out, and their skin turned red. Large swellings containing a watery fluid suddenly appeared on their noses, chins, ears and paws.

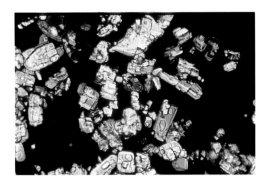

Szent-Györgyi felt that he was on the scent of a hitherto unknown vitamin. In the subsequent course of the experiment, yeast was added to the synthetic feed, whereupon the animals very quickly recovered. Four years later two research groups, one based in America and the other in Germany, almost simultaneously succeeded in identifying the vitamin B6, also called pyridoxine.

Illustration shows vitamin B6

Vitamin B6 regulates protein metabolism

The protein we ingest with our food is almost totally broken down into its individual constituents, the amino acids, as soon as it enters the body. These amino acids are then reassembled into the body's own protein in a number of highly complex processes.

Vitamin B6 has wide-ranging activities: it is involved as a so-called co-enzyme in over 60 enzyme systems of protein and amino-acid metabolism.

Protein is the building material of the body. It is used for the catabolism and maintenance, or renewal of the body substance, rather than for energy production. If vitamin B6 is lacking, the anabolic process stops. Metaphorically speaking, vitamin B6 has a policing role, regulating protein metabolism in the body.

Vitamin B6 deficiency means the whole system suffers

Protein is important for every cell

A functioning protein metabolism is vital for the survival of every cell. Therefore pyridoxine deficiency affects the whole system, and deficiency symptoms manifest themselves in very different organs. The brain and nervous system are especially sensitive to pyridoxine deficiency, because they depend to a great extent on a disturbance-free course of the protein metabolism.

In 1954 in the USA a convulsions epidemic broke out among small children. The cause of this epidemic was a milk preparation for babies which had had its storage stability increased through heating to a high temperature. In doing this, almost the entire B6 content of the milk had been destroyed. This deficiency resulted in the children suffering epileptic-type convulsions. When the affected children were given vitamin B6, the convulsions subsided.

Symptoms of deficiency

Irregular convulsive states are among the typical deficiency symptoms, as are loss of appetite, diarrhoea and vomiting. If pyridoxine is lacking, cutaneous reactions also occur, with inflammation and seborrhoeic rashes around the eyes, mouth and nose and the nervous system shows signs of failure. Pyridoxine deficiency can also cause anaemia, because the first step in the synthesis of the blood pigment – a protein – is dependent upon a pyridoxine-containing co-enzyme.

Source: a ubiquitous vitamin

Vitamin B6 is contained in almost all foods, and is produced both by micro-organisms and by higher plants. Meat and offal have a particularly high pyridoxine content, but a number of fruits and vegetables also contribute well to our intake of the vitamin. Examples of these are potatoes, peas, carrots, green cabbage and beans; top of the list among fruit is bananas. Other very good sources of pyridoxine are bread

Meat, offal, fish

and cereal products. Milk and dairy products, by contrast, contain relatively little vitamin B6. A few species of fish such as mackerel and sardine are also excellent B6 sources, as they contain as much of this vitamin as beef liver.

Recommended daily allowance in adults: 1.6-1.8*mg*

Quantity	Food	Content mg	% of RNI
150g	Salmon	1.47	86%
150g	Chicken liver	1.2	71%
150g	Turkey breast	0.69	41%
150g	Banana, raw	0.55	32%
150g	Avocado, raw	0.8	47%
250g	Potato, raw	0.56	33%
150g	Green/red pepper, raw	0.4	24%
150g	Spinach, sweetcorn	0.33	20%

How much vitamin B6 does our food contain?

Requirement and high-risk groups

The recommended daily amount of pyridoxine in adults ought to be 1.6-1.8mg per day. Notwithstanding its presence in almost all foods, the vitamin B6 intake in some sectors of the population is far from optimal.

Once again, the risk is especially high among young people, particulary younger women between the ages of 18 and 24 years. As in the case of vitamin B2, frequent slimming diets are often thought to be the cause of vitamin B6 deficiency. Pregnant and breast-feeding women also have a higher pyridoxine requirement.

Young people are particularly at risk

• The vitamin B6 requirement is not constant, but can increase, mainly in accordance with the proportion of protein in the diet. People who eat large amounts of meat, fish and dairy products need particularly large quantities of pyridoxine, because animal protein on its own raises the pyridoxine requirement much more markedly than when supplementary protein from vegetables or cereal products is ingested.

Pyridoxine, and pyridoxine antagonists

The contraceptive pill upsets the balance

Continuous use of the contraceptive pill puts a strain on the pyridoxine balance, and also increases the requirement for vitamin B6. In various investigations in women who were on the pill, low vitamin B6 levels and so-called subclinical deficiency symptoms were identified. Some other drugs, such as the tuberculostatic agent, isoniazid, and the antibiotics penicillamine and cycloserine, also have an anti - pyridoxine activity. If these drugs are taken for long periods, an adequate supply of vitamin B6 must be ensured by taking a vitamin supplement.

Drugs and alcohol

As with so many other vitamins, alcohol abuse and heavy smoking also considerably increase the vitamin B6 requirement. These types of addiction are formidable pyridoxine depleters.

Uses of pyridoxine in medicine

Vitamin B6 is used in a great many diseases of the nervous system. In meningitis, concussion and cerebral haemorrhage high doses of vitamin B6 help regenerate damaged nerve cells. Intensive radiation therapy may cause damage, with symptoms such as nausea, vomiting, headache and exhaustion, a sort of radiation-induced hangover. Good results have also been achieved with vitamin B6 in the treatment of this radiation damage. High-dose vitamin B6 is equally effective in myocardial metabolic disturbances brought on by over exertion or excessive sports training, and in some cases of renal impairment or renal insufficiency.

Diseases of the nervous system

Helps treat travel sickness

Vitamin B6 is recommended in a prophylactic dose of 80-200mg to control travel sickness both in humans and when taking domestic pets on long journeys.

Another possible effect of pyridoxine is currently still at the research stage. In Cuba, where sugar cane forms part of the staple diet, it has been discovered that children very rarely suffer from tooth decay. Scientists think that the high vitamin B6 content of sugar cane has a protective function against tooth decay.

No side-effects or actual symptoms of disease resulting from high doses of vitamin B6 are known to date.

Vitamin B12 – keeps our blood young

People suffering from vitamin B12 deficiency have a pale and bloodless appearance. Until the beginning of the twentieth century, when the cause of pernicious anaemia was not yet known, thousands of people died from this now easily-cured disease. In the 1920s an American doctor, George Minot, had an idea which brought the first ray of hope for people suffering from this disease.

His theory was that the disease occurred only in people with a diseased or damaged liver. His prescribed therapy was a mixture of raw liver, a little lemon, onions and various herbs, all minced and mixed together well. Although many patients experienced an improvement in their symptoms, most reacted with nausea at the unappetising sight of the raw liver.

Illustration shows vitamin B12

These modest results at least set scientists on the right track, and in 1934 Dr. Minot received the Nobel prize for his work. Cobalamin, the chemical name for vitamin B12, was not discovered until 14 years later: in 1948 a generous 1g of a red, crystalline liquid was isolated for the first time from 4000kg of liver. This liquid was cobalamin.

Vitamin B12 for haematopoiesis and growth
Although cobalamin is not involved in all reactions in the body, those in which it does play a role are the more important ones. Vitamin B12 is needed so that the red blood cells can be continually formed in the bone marrow throughout our life span. In the absence of cobalamin, certain basal reactions in the metabolism of carbohydrate, fat and protein will not take place. Unfortunately, these reactions are necessary for a great many vital processes.

A lack of vitamin B12 impairs growth so an adequate supply of this vitamin is particularly important for small children and adolescents.

Vitamin B12 is necessary wherever the body needs to regenerate a large number of cells in a short space of time – for example in the nervous system, where it is involved in the formation of nerve tissue.

Deficiency leads to pernicious anaemia

Destructive anaemia is a description often given to pernicious anaemia, the classical vitamin B12 deficiency disease. This was dreaded long before the discovery of the vitamin because at that time, the disease was indeed destructive. Because there was no known cure the outcome was usually the death of the patient.

The outwardly visible symptom is a pale yellow skin coloration; other symptoms are extreme tiredness and exhaustion, inflamed tongue, tingling of the limbs, and even paralysis. The biochemical signs are identified under the microscope as severe cellular alterations, particularly in the cells of the haematopoietic (blood-producing) system.

Only in very rare cases is severe cobalamin deficiency due to malnutrition. The usual reasons are digestive disorders such as chronic gastritis or diseases of the small intestine such as diverticulosis. Drugs and toxins too can induce pernicious anaemia, for example certain anticonvulsants, tuberculostatics, as well as some antibiotics, such as neomycin and colchicine.

Most of these causes trigger the cobalamin deficiency by the same mechanism: they block the uptake of the vitamin into the body from the intestine. Cobalamin is introduced into the metabolism exclusively via an active transport mechanism. The transporting agent is an intrinsic factor, a substance produced by special cells in the stomach. If the intrinsic factor is absent, or if its formation is disturbed or for some reason actually ceases – as for example in chronic gastritis – vitamin B12 is no longer absorbed into the body.

Sources and availability

For our vitamin B12 requirement, humans and animals alike must rely on bacteria, for only they are able to produce cobalamin compounds. Whether humans are capable of absorbing and utilizing the cobalamin produced by our own intestinal bacteria is not entirely clear. Apparently minimal quantities can be absorbed, but these are too low to meet the body's requirement.

Animal produce

The best source of vitamin B12 is animal produce; liver, kidneys and brain have a particularly high content. Other good sources are milk and dairy products, lean meat, fish and eggs. Beer and sauerkraut, which are both end-products of fermentation processes which are started by bacteria, also contain small quantities of the vitamin. Vitamin B12 is water-soluble and sensitive to heat, and is largely destroyed during cooking.

Vitamin B12 and vitamin C provide an example of the damaging relationship that can exist between some vitamins: cobalamin can be destroyed by an excess of vitamin C. Vitamin B1 has a negative influence on the stability of vitamin B12. There are also a number of interactions between cobalamin and various drugs. For example, the contraceptive pill lowers the vitamin B12 level in the blood, while drugs to treat tuberculosis, and anticonvulsant agents inhibit the absorption of cobalamin from the intestine.

Harmful interactions

Requirement and high-risk groups

The recommended nutrient intake suggests that an intake of 1.5µg per day is sufficient for our needs. A well-balanced, varied diet contains vitamin B12 in quantities far in excess of our requirement. Losses during food preparation, often as a result of frying or high-temperature roasting of meat or fish, or the boiling of milk, can vary between 10-30% of the vitamin B12 content. This means that even cooking at high temperatures has virtually no effect on our intake. As little as half a pint of milk a day, 10g of calf's liver or two eggs are sufficient to prevent deficiency in the long-term.

Even if there are serious disturbances of the vitamin B12 intake or inadequate nutrition, manifest deficiency phenomena normally arise only after a matter of years. The body's cobalamin reserves amount to around 2-5g, most of which is stored in the liver and which, even if the intake were to cease totally, would be sufficient to last for at least 1,000 days.

The only really high-risk group are strict vegetarians, or vegans, who exclude not only meat, but also milk, dairy products and eggs from their diet. This means that they actually do not eat anything which contains cobalamin. All the same, for the reasons already mentioned, even in this group severe deficiency states are extremely rare. However, there could be a serious risk to wholly breast-fed babies of vegan mothers.

Vegetarians and vegans could be at risk

Recommended daily allowance in adults: 1.5μ**g**

How much vitamin B12 does our food contain?

Quantity	Food	Content μg	% of RNI
10g	Calf's liver	6	200%
50g	Herring	4.25	142%
100g	Salmon	2.9	97%
150g	Joint of beef	3.3	110%
500g	Milk	2.1	70%
175g	Yoghurt	0.75	25%
125g	Quark, low-fat	1.1	37%
30g	Camembert	0.93	31%

Uses of vitamin B12 in medicine

Neuralgia and neuritis are frequently treated with drug combinations which, in addition to the vitamins B1 and B6, also contain large amounts of vitamin B12. Owing to their positive effects on the nerve cells, doctors also call these neurotropic vitamins.

Biotin – the elixir of life for the skin

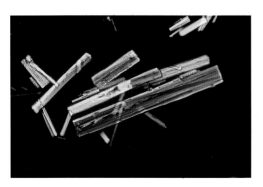

Bios, meaning 'life', was the name given at the beginning of the twentieth century to the still unidentified active substance which yeast needs for growth. Not until 35 years later did the German chemists, Kögl and Tönnis, succeed in isolating biotin from egg yolks and analysing its structure.

Illustration shows biotin

Biotin functions as a carbon dioxide carrier

The substance which fuels the metabolism, the engine that supplies us with energy, is glucose. Glucose is manufactured continuously from carbohydrates in our diet and, if necessary, even from fats in a process which is called gluconeogenesis. If the metabolism lacks biotin, gluconeogenesis is interrupted.

The task of biotin in this process is to supply carbon dioxide, which is required for glucose production. Carbon dioxide is either used or liberated in many of the chemical reactions of our metabolism, such as anabolism of the fats, proteins and carbohydrates of the body – in these cases biotin acts as it were as a carrier, conveying the gas from one place to another.

On the other hand, biotin is also required for the catabolism of many substances – for example for the splitting up of various amino acids in protein catabolism. This gives an idea of the importance of biotin for growth and the renewal of blood, nerves, skin and hair.

Deficiency: the skin is the first thing to suffer

The first indications of biotin deficiency were revealed in experiments with rats fed a diet of raw protein. The symptoms were inflammation of the skin, hair loss and reproductive disorders.

Similarly in studies using human volunteers who ate raw
egg-white for a lengthy period, the first alterations occurred
in the skin. After three to four weeks, the skin began to
exfoliate severely; this developed into severe dermatitis,
accompanied by depression, tiredness, myalgia, loss of
appetite and nausea. The symptoms disappeared
completely within five days of the correction of the
imbalance with an injection of biotin. It is easy to explain
why biotin deficiency is triggered by raw egg. The raw white
of hens' eggs contains avidin; this substance has the
adverse characteristic of bonding chemically with all the
biotin available from food, with the result that our digestive
system can no longer utilize it. Heat destroys avidin,
however, and lovers of dishes made with eggs have no
need to worry because avidin is inactivated when eggs are
boiled or baked.

Avidin – an
adverse
factor in raw
egg

Sources and availability
Like cobalamin, biotin is mainly produced by micro-
organisms. Almost all foods contain traces of biotin, the
majority of them only in quantities of a few millionths of a
gram. Liver and yeast have the highest biotin content.

Large
amounts are
contained in
liver and
yeast

The human intestinal flora also produce biotin but, as in
the case of cobalamin, once again it is not known for certain
whether this intestinal biotin can actually be utilized.

Requirement and high-risk groups
Current recommendations for our intake of biotin are based
exclusively on estimates. From a normal, varied diet we
absorb between 50-100µg of biotin per day and, since no
diet-related deficiency phenomena have so far been
observed in association with this quantity, the
recommended intake is 30-100µg of biotin per day.

As with the other vitamins, there are some groups
whose requirements are different to the recommended
daily amount. For example, people who believe that raw
eggs are healthy can do their biotin intake just as much
harm as a chronic alcoholic with cirrhosis of the liver, who
often have an extremely low blood biotin concentration.

Recommended daily allowance in adults: 30-100µg

Quantity	Food	Content µg	% of RNI
500g	Fresh milk (1.5; 3.5%)	17.5	27%
100g	Calf's liver	75	115%
100g	Lamb's kidney	55	85%

Uses of biotin in medicine

Biotin deficiency states are frequently observed in patients who have to be fed by infusion for several months because of some serious disorder. The reason for this is that biotin is absent from many infusion solutions even though, as a vital nutrient, they should all contain it.

Niacin – ensures our energy supply

Niacin consists of two substances with vitamin-like activity: nicotinic acid and nicotinamide, which are mutually interchangeable in the metabolism.

Illustration shows niacin

• Although niacin is chemically related to nicotine, in its activity it has nothing at all in common with this toxin.

Niacin functions as a hydrogen carrier

Niacin is to hydrogen what biotin is to carbon dioxide. Just as carbon dioxide is split off or accumulated in many anabolic or catabolic physical processes, the same thing happens with hydrogen in many stages of energy production. Niacin is converted in the body into its active forms, nicotinamide-adenine dinucleotide (NAD) and nicotinamide-adenine dinucleotide phosphate (NADP). These two substances act as hydrogen-donating or hydrogen-accepting co-enzymes in more than 200 biochemical metabolic reactions. Niacin is especially important in all the processes involved in energy production.

Niacin has a special status among vitamins, because we are dependent upon its intake with the food we eat to a limited extent. Nutritional protein is composed of amino acids; our metabolism is able to manufacture niacin from the degradation of one of these amino acids, tryptophan. This means that the cause of niacin deficiency can, in most cases, be traced to protein deficiency.

Niacin deficiency leads to pellagra

Pellagra was, and still is, a disease of poor and undernourished people of the Third World. It arises in areas where the diet of the population consists almost exclusively of maize and the species of millet called sorghum. Maize is extremely deficient in tryptophan and the niacin in maize is present in a chemical compound which cannot be utilized by the body.

Symptoms of deficiency

The symptoms of pellagra include: dermatitis, when the skin becomes inflamed and covered with dark patches, keratinizes, and eventually flakes off; diarrhoea which is associated with loss of appetite, vomiting, and inflammation of the stomach and tongue and dementia. Dementia is where neurological disturbances, which initially take the form of tiredness, dizziness and headache, may eventually include depression, confusion and uncontrolled muscular twitching. In our part of the world, niacin deficiency only ever occurs as a consequence of severe alcoholism or digestive disturbances which prevent the uptake of niacin by the body.

If maize is roasted or immersed in lime-water, the niacin is released from its chemical bond and can be absorbed and processed by the body. In some Indian tribes found in Central America, knowledge of this method for preventing niacin deficiency is part of the store of wisdom that has been passed down over the ages, from one generation to the next.

Sources and availability

Niacin also resembles biotin in its occurrence: niacin occurs widely in foodstuffs of both plant and vegetable origin, although in most foods it is present only in very small amounts. Especially good sources of niacin are liver, yeast, heart, kidneys and lean meat. Coffee beans also have a high niacin content, which is then further increased by roasting.

Niacin is present in coffee beans

Since the tryptophan-rich foods are essentially also important suppliers of niacin, the niacin content of a food is, as a rule, stated in niacin equivalents – it comprises the quantity of niacin which can be converted from the tryptophan content of the food in question. Milk and eggs, for example, contain almost no niacin, but they do have a high tryptophan content and are therefore important suppliers of niacin.

Niacin is not sensitive to either light or temperature. The greatest losses occur from leaching, for example as a result of boiling vegetables in too much water, when 15-25% of the niacin originally present ends up in the cooking water.

Our diet usually satisfies our niacin requirement

In this part of the world, diet-related niacin deficiency is not a problem, as the recommended daily amount of niacin is met from our usual varied diet. This is quite apart from the fact that we are eating more food rich in egg-white than ever before, and can therefore supply a high proportion of the niacin requirement from the tryptophan in our diet.

Niacin from tryptophan

The niacin requirement is 18mg niacin equivalent per day for men, and 15mg niacin equivalent per day for women. The requirement is higher for pregnant and breast-feeding women – 17mg and 20mg respectively. Adolescents between the ages of 15 and 19 years require 20mg for males and 16mg for females.

Because niacin plays a role in the availability of energy, the requirement is always increased whenever more than the average amount of energy is needed, for example during active sports or when doing heavy physical work. The requirement is also higher in people who are overweight, those having a course of febrile infections or people with digestive disturbances, as well as during phases of physical growth. A number of drugs block the utilization of niacin and may, if taken for long periods or in cases of chronic drug abuse, lead to deficiency, a particular risk when taking certain analgesics, or psychotropic drugs containing diazepam.

As the energy requirement increases, so does the need for niacin

How much niacin does our food contain?

Recommended daily allownce in adults: 15–18mg

Quantity	Food	Content mg	% of RNI
150g	Mackerel	11.55	70%
150g	Chicken breast	15.75	95%
150g	Escalope of veal	11.25	68%
150g	Ham	5.25	32%
200g	Green peas, raw	5.8	35%
150g	Mushrooms	7.05	43%

Uses of niacin in medicine

Niacin is an important ingredient in many medicines, as it is beneficial in a number of diseases:

- in various severe diarrhoeal diseases and digestive disorders, for example sprue;
- in the treatment of schizophrenia, owing to its positive effects on the nervous system;
- in circulatory disorders, hypertension, asthma, various forms of anaemia, arthritis and skin diseases as a supporting active substance in high doses of at least 3g niacin;
- in the treatment of hypercholesterolaemia and the harmful LDL blood lipids. High-dose niacin reduces the cholesterol concentration by as much as 30%. However, anyone wishing to improve their circulation and reduce their elevated blood lipid concentration should be careful not to let ingestion of preparations with a high niacin content get out of control.

Even small quantities of niacin lead many patients to side effects which, although not life-threatening, are nevertheless very unpleasant. Almost half of all patients prescribed niacin preparations discontinue the treatment prematurely for this reason. Side-effects range from vasodilation with pronounced reddening of the skin, severe pruritus and hot flushes, through to gastritis, disturbances of liver function, and a decline in blood pressure.

Niacin has many possible uses

Unpleasant side-effects

Pantothenic acid – for healthy skin and hair

'Anti-greying factor', 'chicken dermatitis factor', 'protective factor X' are just some of the names which have been given to pantothenic acid in the past. They all originate from the early history of this vitamin.

Illustration shows pantothenic acid

Deficiency phenomena were first discovered in animals, including rats, whose fur turns grey when the vitamin is absent from the diet and chickens, which develop an inflammation of the skin as a result of pantothenic-acid deficiency.

However, it was not until 1940 that an American scientist, called Harris, analysed the chemical structure of pantothenic acid.

Without pantothenic acid nothing works properly

Coenzyme A is the name given to a substance which fulfils a sort of traffic-controlling function during many chemical reactions of protein, fat and carbohydrate metabolism; coenzyme A mediates these reactions, which take place only in its presence.

Coenzyme A is produced from pantothenic acid in five stages of transformation. One substance required for this process is vitamin B6. This is an example of the way in which the activity of different vitamins can be seen to work together through influencing one another at different sites within the body.

Coenzyme A is another substance whose function is essentially to act as a carrier, in this case in the transfer of acetic acid. The acetic acid-coenzyme A compound is also regarded as the very centre of the metabolism, as it represents an end point of carbohydrate, fat and protein metabolism.

Pantothenic acid deficiency is very rare

A typical deficiency disease like the ones which are characteristic of many other vitamins is unknown in the case of pantothenic acid.

Symptoms of deficiency

Under experimental conditions, volunteer test subjects ingested a substance which destroyed the pantothenic acid in the diet. The effects of this artificially induced deficiency were tiredness, disturbances of sleep and balance, nausea and vomiting, tremor of the hands, and muscle cramps. In animal experiments, the pantothenic-acid deficiency led to impaired growth, weight loss, damage to fur and feathers, disorders of the nervous system including paralysis, persistent diarrhoea, and inhibition of antibody formation.

Sources and availability

Pantothenic acid, from Greek 'pantothen' meaning 'from every side', occurs in almost all foods. Offal, some kinds of meat, and various types of cereal are particularly rich sources of pantothen.

Our supply is generally good

Since pantothenic acid is soluble in water and sensitive to heat, losses of up to 30% must be expected during the food preparation stage. However, the high intake in a normal diet means that in the case of pantothenic acid, such losses are relatively easily tolerated.

Requirement and high-risk groups

Because diet-induced deficiency never really occurs, the requirements data are also largely based on estimates. The recommended daily allowance is 6mg per day. This quantity is assumed to ensure an adequate intake in adults of all ages and adolescents over 13 years of age: some investigations have actually demonstrated that even with a daily intake of only 1mg of pantothen, no deficiency phenomena occur.

Stress increases the requirement

Stress increases the pantothen requirement, because the vitamin plays a role in the formation of the stress hormone in the adrenals. However, it is thought that the recommended 6mg per day is even sufficient in extreme conditions of stress.

Recommended daily allowance in adults: 6mg

Quantity	Food	Content mg	% of RNI	
150	Herring	1.2	20%	
100g	Calf's liver	7.9		132%
200g	Asparagus, raw	1.24	21%	
200g	Broccoli, raw	2.02	34%	
150g	Water melon	2.4	40%	
150g	Mushrooms	3.15	53%	

Uses of pantothen in medicine

Pantothen is an ingredient in a whole range of ointments, for example eye and nose ointments, and ointments for wound healing. This is because it is easily absorbed by skin and mucosae, and can reach deeper skin layers, where it is then pharmacologically active. Pantothenic acid also appears to have a positive effect on wound repair when used internally. Some studies have demonstrated that high doses of this vitamin accelerate post-surgical wound repair and simultaneously prevent excessively prominent, bulky scars.

Pantothen
promotes
wound
healing

Pantothenic acid is also used for the treatment of psychological disturbances and nervous disorders and to stimulate intestinal motility following surgery. Its efficacy in these applications has not yet been confirmed, however.

Folic acid – a key role in cell division

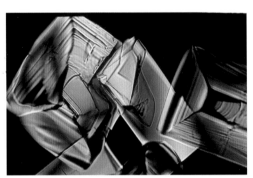

For a long time folic acid led something of a behind-the-scenes existence. However, in recent years, the research carried out by scientists has pushed the vitamin more and more into the limelight. One reason is that the intake of a number of population subgroups falls seriously short of the requirement; the other is that it is now known that the vitamin plays an important role in the development of the foetus during the first three months of pregnancy.

Illustration shows folic acid

Folic acid is essential for blood formation and cell growth

Folic acid is needed wherever the cells of the body divide and multiply. Growth and maturation of the red blood cells – a lifelong process – can only function smoothly in the presence of adequate folic acid. Here, folic acid is the active partner of vitamin B12, which is equally essential for haematopoiesis or blood formation.

Folic acid is primarily involved in protein metabolism, and its particular importance is also due to its influence on the production of deoxyribonucleic acid (DNA) and ribonucleic acid (RNA), which are the carriers and transfer agents of all our genetic material. Their production is impossible without folic acid.

Folic acid deficiency damages the growing organism

In the bone marrow, which is where blood cells are produced, new cells are constantly and extensively being formed. The bone marrow's folic acid consumption is correspondingly high, and it is here that a deficiency of folic acid first manifests itself.

The first
symptom of
deficiency is
anaemia

The signs of deficiency are similar to those of a vitamin B12 deficit: anaemia, with inflated, excessively large blood cells known as megaloblasts. The mucosae are also affected; this manifests itself as alterations in the cells of the lungs, bronchi, bladder and uterus. Severe folic acid deficiency can result in infertility in both sexes. In view of the fact that folic acid deficiency is so widespread, couples who have not been able to have a child should always have the folic acid levels in their blood checked.

• Folic acid deficiency can have serious consequences for an existing pregnancy and for the foetus. Miscarriages and certain malformations, such as spina bifida, are directly linked to folic acid deficiency. Other damage to the embryo and premature delivery can also be as a result of severe folic acid deficiency.

The
requirement
is higher
during
pregnancy

Sources and availability:
The name folic acid is derived from 'folium', a Latin word meaning 'leaf'. This may be because many varieties of lettuce and leafy green vegetables have very high folic acid contents. This includes spinach, endives, kale and hearting lettuce. Beetroot, cauliflower and wholemeal products are also good suppliers of folic acid, although the vitamin also occurs in animal produce. With the exception of liver and kidneys, which are among the foods which contain the highest amount of folic acid, the folic acid content of meat is relatively low.

Eat plenty of
leafy green
vegetables

Only about 25% of the folic acid in our diet is available in the free form – this unbound substance is absorbed from the intestine. Most of the folic acid is present in compounds as the folate, only about half of which can be used.

The situation regarding folic acid is the same as for some other vitamins: the existence of different compounds with activity as the vitamin is the reason why the amount contained in foods and the recommended intakes are given in folic acid equivalents. These take account of the differences in the extent to which the various compound forms can be utilised.

A highly sensitive vitamin

Folic acid is highly sensitive to influences during food preparation. It is soluble in water, light-sensitive and extremely sensitive to heat. If lettuce is soaked for too long, vegetables are boiled in too much water, or meat or liver is fried or roasted at too high a temperature, considerable losses of folic acid occur. Even cooking methods such as steaming with very little water, or cooking in a clay pot or microwave, are insufficient to preserve the folic acid.

Requirement and high-risk groups

Folic acid is a crucial vitamin. Various investigations have shown that the physical requirement is not properly safeguarded in a large sector of the population. The recommended allowance of µg of folic acid per day is very difficult to achieve from a daily diet rich in meat and fats. Groups at particular risk are:

• Pregnant women; because their folic acid requirement is twice as high as normal (while their energy requirement is only about 20% above normal). The reason for this is that the growing embryo uses up enormous quantities of the vitamin. The risk is especially high in women with a multiple pregnancy. It is almost impossible to cover the additional folic acid requirement during this period from the diet alone, so a folic acid supplement is certainly advisable.

• Breast-feeding women; the folic acid requirement of this group is still 50% above normal, because the baby needs large amounts of the vitamin for growth and gets its entire requirement from its mother's milk. The folate reserves of babies born prematurely are particularly low, which also means that a breast-feeding mother needs a good supply of folic acid to be able to compensate for the deficiency in the baby.

• Children; they need sufficient folic acid, especially during phases of growth, in order to ensure cellular proliferation and optimal cell growth. Investigations have shown that the folic acid supply of many young people is particularly poor during puberty on account of the growth spurt.

Folic acid for growth

• Alcoholics; an extremely low folic acid level in this group is primarily attributable to their diet. Alcoholics get most of their calories in liquid form, as 'empty' calories. Alcohol also seems to impair the utilization of folic acid, even at the biochemical level.

A good supply from fruit and vegetables

To meet our folic acid requirement from our daily diet we need to eat highly nutritious foods. Raw vegetables, fruit such as oranges and bananas, which are rich in folic acid, and wholemeal products are the best foods for ensuring that the daily requirement is covered.

How much folic acid does our food contain?

Recommended daily allowance in adults: 225μg

Quantity	Food	Content μg	% of RNI
150g	Pig's liver	360	160%
200g	Curly kale, raw	180	80%
150g	Sprouts, spinach, raw	117	52%
150g	Beetroot, raw	140	63%
100g	Beans	130	58%
100g	Chick-peas	200	89%
20g	Wheat-germ	104	46%
200 g	Wholewheat bread	120	53%

Use of folic acid in medicine

Folic acid in a pharmaceutical form is used almost exclusively to prevent the consequences of folic acid deficiency in pregnant or breast-feeding women and in cases of folic acid-induced anaemia. It is also used to treat malnutrition-induced folic acid deficiency in alcoholics, individuals with diseases of the gastrointestinal tract, and in patients whose folic acid supply is at risk due to drug interactions.

Prevention of deficiency

• Many drugs, for example anticonvulsants and contraceptives, will impair the availability of folic acid for use by the body.

Vitamin C – strengthens the immune system

The oldest description of vitamin C deficiency disease comes from a papyrus dating from the second century BC. Scurvy was the scourge of countless seafarers, navigators,

warriors and crusaders. All they usually had to eat on their interminable voyages was a meagre, unbalanced diet, which tended to make them ill, so that at the end many suffered a wretched death. In the seventeenth century it was discovered that the disease could be prevented with fruit and fresh vegetables. However, it was another three hundred years before scientists managed to discover the exact chemical designation and analysis of vitamin C.

Illustration
shows
vitamin C

Vitamin C mobilizes the body's defence mechanism

Chemically known as ascorbic acid, vitamin C acts as an oxidation agent. It is one of the 'carrier' vitamins which transports substances such as oxygen and hydrogen. The activity of vitamin C as a scavenger of free radicals (see page 24) is also due to its ability to bind free oxygen to itself. This property, which has attracted a lot of interest in scientific circles in recent years, is the basis of the role of ascorbic acid in protecting against cancer, arteriosclerosis and myocardial infarction. In addition, vitamin C also fulfils a large number of routine functions in the body:

• Anabolism and regeneration of connective tissue. In practice an obvious example of this is wound repair and cicatrization – without vitamin C wound healing and scar formation will not take place.

• Absorption and utilization of the important trace elements in the body. Vitamin C improves the absorption of iron from the intestine, and helps continuously replenish the iron stores in liver, spleen and bone marrow.

Promotes the
formation of
antibodies

• Vitamin C stimulates the defence activities of the white blood cells in the immune system, and promotes the formation of antibodies.

• Vitamin C plays an important, albeit as yet imprecisely clarified role in overcoming stress. The adrenal cortex protects us in stressful situations by releasing hormones – the corticosteroids. Simultaneously, the vitamin C reserves of the adrenal cortex are rapidly emptied. This explains why the vitamin C levels of people who are permanently under a lot of strain are often severely depleted. Involvement in the production of these endogenous cortisones is presumably also the basis of another beneficial property of vitamin C; the improved protection against infections.

Protects
against
infection

• Vitamin C assists with detoxification processes in the liver, for example after taking drugs.

• Ascorbic acid inhibits the formation of carcinogenic nitrosamines in the stomach from nitrate in food: the gastric mucosa releases vitamin C after every meal, apparently for this purpose.

A number of investigations suggest that vitamin C also lowers the cholesterol level, but confirmation is still awaited both for this, and for a great many other positive effects which it apparently has on the body's immune system.

Deficiency: the trouble starts with bleeding gums

Scurvy, the classical vitamin C deficiency disease, is manifested in the first instance in seemingly harmless early symptoms such as tiredness, irritability, increased requirement for sleep, pains in the joints and limbs and impaired physical ability. Bleeding from the skin and mucosae, and bleeding gums are typical and are the first objective signs of the threat of scurvy. As the development of the disease progresses, this is followed by alterations affecting the bones and joints, previously-healed wounds re-open, the teeth fall out and susceptibility to infection is greatly increased. In the past, scurvy sufferers frequently died of quite commonplace infections against which the body could no longer offer any resistance.

Symptoms of
deficiency

Sources and availability

Fruit, fresh vegetables and freshly-pressed fruit and vegetable juices are the most important suppliers of vitamin C; tropical fruits and berries have a particularly high vitamin C content. Top of the list is the blackcurrant: 100g of this fruit yields two and a half times the recommended daily allowance. Other important sources of vitamin C are oranges, kiwis, strawberries, raspberries and redcurrants, as well as exotic fruits such as mango and papaya.

Blackcurrants are the No. 1 supplier of vitamin C

Of the vegetables, paprika, broccoli, brussels sprouts and cauliflower contain especially large amounts of vitamin C, but potatoes, leeks and tomatoes also deserve acknowledgement as suppliers of the vitamin. In foods of animal origin, only liver has a reasonable vitamin C content.

How much vitamin C is absorbed by the body depends on the ingested dose. The larger the vitamin intake, the less – relatively speaking – is absorbed from the intestine. This means that any excess is immediately excreted via the kidneys. Moreover, as for other vitamins there are a number of factors which restrict the availability of vitamin C: the contraceptive pill and other drugs such as sulphonamides can considerably impair the utilization of the vitamin.

Excesses are excreted

Requirement and high-risk groups

Scurvy can be prevented with a daily dose of as little as 10mg vitamin C per day. However, this cannot be described as the optimum intake. The recommended daily allowances are as follows: including a good safety margin adolescents and adults need 75mg of vitamin C per day, and pregnant and breast-feeding women 100mg and 125mg per day respectively.

Like all the other water-soluble vitamins, vitamin C can only be stored in small amounts. Even with the full storage capacity in the liver, adrenals, brain and lungs, the body's total reserves amount to only 3g. To keep the reserves constantly full to the brim, our intake would have to be about 200mg per day. Although it has not been confirmed whether it is necessary for the body's reserves to be constantly replenished before the vitamin can express its optimum activity, in view of the presumed effects of the vitamin – protection from cancer, arteriosclerosis and myocardial infarction, stimulation of the immune system and protection against infections – taking an extra 100-150mg vitamin C per day seems a small price to pay for so great a return.

Several fundamentally at-risk groups have to take care to ensure that they get a particularly good supply of vitamin C: smokers, people suffering from chronic stress, pregnant and breast-feeding women, the elderly and people with a weak constitution have a higher requirement (see High-risk groups, page 87; Vitamin depleters, page 92), as do people who take part in active sports, and those who are exposed to severe physical strain.

Groups at risk

Uses of vitamin C in medicine

We are frequently advised to begin taking high-dose vitamin C for colds and flu, even after the onset of the infection. But the efficacy of this is debatable. These so-called vitamin C intervention treatments are even attempted in cancer cases. Serious scientists are, however, agreed that it is pointless to treat cancer with vitamin C. What is important is to ensure that we get the best possible vitamin C intake, for vitamin C is the basis of, and essential for, a well-functioning immune system in its activity of resisting and fighting disease.

Preventive vitamin

How much vitamin C does our food contain?

Recommended daily allowance in adults: 75mg

Quantity	Food	Content mg	% of RNI
200g	Potatoes, raw	44	59%
200g	Asparagus, raw	56	75%
150g	White cabbage, raw	70.5	94%
100g	Brussel sprouts, raw	102	136%
100g	Broccoli, raw	110	147%
50g	Green/red peppers, raw	70	93%
100g	Grapefruit, raw	41	55%
100g	Strawberries, raw	62	83%
50g	Kiwi, raw	75	100%
20g	Blackcurrants.	57	76%

Pseudovitamins – substances which act in a similar way to vitamins

In addition to the 13 vitamins described, a great many other substances behave in a way similar to vitamins: these are the pseudovitamins. As a rule they act like true vitamins but, unlike the latter, they can usually be manufactured by the body itself and no typical deficiency phenomena can be demonstrated. Repeated attempts are now being made to market certain substances by using the healthy image of vitamins to make an even healthier profit.

Substances with vitamin-like properties

Vitamin Q10 is an excellent example of a substance which the body is perfectly capable of manufacturing itself, yet which is being promoted as the 'heart vitamin' or 'the high-performance vitamin'. In fact, Q10 is not even a pseudovitamin! According to the promotional material and a few published reports, Q10 – a coenzyme – strengthens the heart and immune system, reduces high blood pressure, and prolongs life.

Claims of this nature are both premature and, on the basis of current knowledge, untenable. Advice to the effect that coenzyme Q10 has a vitamin-like character and should be taken as a dietary supplement are media hype for which there is no conclusive evidence. This is an example of a substance being elevated to the status of vitamin by marketing experts.

Coenzyme Q10

Coenzyme Q10, also known as ubiquinone, is indeed present in all human cells, where it is vitally important for the availability of energy. Positive effects, for example on the heart and circulation, certainly are known. The only thing is, the body is capable of manufacturing adequate amounts of ubiquinone itself so that supplements are not required.

Ester C and Super C are respectively the trade mark and trade name under which a new vitamin is being introduced, supposedly heralding an associated revolution in vitamin therapy. Ester C is not even a substance which, from the point of view of its chemistry, can be classed as a pseudovitamin; rather, it is a new product from an American pharmaceutical company, in which vitamin C is mixed with excipients which allegedly improve its utilization in the body. Claims that this product is the most effective of all known substances against viruses, and also blocks all known mechanisms leading to cancer, heart disease and arthritis must far exceed the bounds of credibility.

Vitamin F is another falsely-named substance. The unsaturated fatty acids, above all linoleic acid, are still being erroneously designated vitamin F in many different publications. While it is true that the essential fatty acids have to be obtained from outside the body and ingested in the diet, something which they have in common with vitamins, in the body they do not function as an active substance, but as a structural material, for example as an elementary constituent of the cell membrane. For this reason they are not vitamins. However, the intention behind their being called a vitamin is, in most cases, to promote these substances using the positive image of vitamins.

The substance class of the pseudovitamins also contains a great many other substances; some of the most important ones are listed below:

• Choline can be manufactured in the liver, and also occurs in small quantities in cereals, meat and vegetables. It is required, among other things, for the manufacture of acetylcholine in nerve tissue, and is therefore an important factor for the functioning of stimulus conduction.

• Bioflavonoids are plant constituents for which vitamin-like activity is constantly being claimed, although deficiency phenomena have never been demonstrated. The most well-known of the flavonoids is probably rutin, which is available in tablet form and which is said to be beneficial for haemorrhagic tendencies and varicose veins.

• Orotic acid is occasionally recommended as a drug which is believed to increase the excretion of uric acid by the kidneys, for example in cases of gout.

• Pangamic acid is considered to be a miracle drug in the USA which improves the circulation and stimulates the oxygen supply.

It is worth remembering that all these claims have yet to be proved!

Inositol is a carbohydrate which in deficiency triggers growth disturbances in some animal species. In humans it is said to be important for normal gastrointestinal function, and it is recommended as a curative agent in some liver complaints. However, there is no evidence that inositol is essential in humans, and in any case it can be produced in the body.

Laetrile, also called vitamin B17, has a reputation as an effective anticancer drug, particularly in the USA. It is highly toxic in large doses. In the USA, numerous cases of poisoning and several deaths have ocurred as a result of laetrile overdose.

Other substances said to have vitamin-like activity

• Caution should always be exercised in respect of substances which are not among the 13 classical vitamins, but are nevertheless claimed as vitamins; these substances do more for the economic well-being of the manufacturer than the health of the consumer!

High-risk groups have higher requirements

Malnutrition
is possible
even if food is
available in
excess

It is possible to have a vitamin deficiency despite an apparently healthy diet. This is because even when food is available in excess, malnutrition is still possible through eating the wrong things. In fact bad eating habits are probably the commonest reason for vitamin deficiency. Nutritonists now know that very specific groups of people are affected:

• Children and adolescents, pregnant or breast-feeding women, and the elderly. These groups are in a phase of life in which the requirement for nutrients and vitamins is especially high.

Requirement
is higher
during certain
phases of life

• Sick people and convalescents, individuals on long-term medication, strict vegetarians, people who frequently go on crash diets, and the socially disadvantaged are also at risk of vitamin deficiency on account of their personal circumstances or lifestyle.

Use of the word 'deficiency' to describe this situation does not imply that true deficiency disease is imminent. 'Deficiency' is used here to describe situations where the daily vitamin intake is below the recommended amount, or is giving rise to subclinical deficiency phenomena such as listlessness, impaired ability to perform, and tiredness. Even mild deficiency should not be underestimated. If compounded by other stress factors such as illness, the supply of vitamins can rapidly become critical.

The sections below reveal the position in the case of the most important high-risk groups.

Children and adolescents

Scanty health
awareness

The vitamin intake among adolescents leaves much to be desired. Many investigations suggest that folic acid, vitamin B2 and thiamine and, more rarely, vitamin A may be regarded as crucial nutrients in this age group. The vitamin C and vitamin D intakes of many adolescents are similarly below par. Of course, young people should have their fun, but smoking, which raises the consumption of vitamins C and E and folic acid, sex, which requires a higher vitamin E, vitamin B6, folic acid and vitamin C consumption if the pill is being taken, and alcohol all increase the vitamin consumption required by this group.

Eating is a secondary or substitute activity

This is not helped by the fact that many young people tend to give little thought to eating the right foods. They eat less salad, vegetables, fruit and bread than previous generations, and eat more chocolate, sweets and sugar, put more salt on their food and consume more soft drinks. Some of these bad habits become reflected in the critical biochemical values of the nutrient requirement levels.

• A nutritious diet including lots of fruit and vegetables, wholemeal products, milk and dairy products not only provides a good vitamin supply, but is also good for our health and our overall mood.

Young women

No other population subgroup contains such a high proportion of underweight individuals as the group of young women within the age range 18-24 years. The reason for this is that, for many women of this age group, having the ideal figure means being over-thin. By the age of 20 they

Diet-induced deficiency

have frequently had several attempts at dieting. It is hardly surprising that this leads to malnutrition, with consequences for the vitamin supply. Their intake imbalances – above all vitamin B2 and folic acid – are greater than those of people in any other phase of life. Consequently they are even more at risk than the elderly or pregnant women, although pregnancy in women in this age-group can further greatly increase the risk. The vitamin A, B1 and E intake is also less than satisfactory in these women.

Dieting adversely affects the vitamin intake

Continual dieting has a yo-yo effect. The body adapts to the need for greater economies with the calories, and uses the food more and more efficiently. After this sort of dieting, the weight increases all the faster. The only real alternative is a calorie-reduced varied diet, based on nutritious food, with 1,500-1,800 calories per day. Weight is lost slowly, steadily, and without hunger pangs. Careful selection of the food we eat also ensures a good supply of vitamins.

The elderly

The reclusive lifestyle of many elderly people influences their vitamin intake in a negative way; problems which require attention are deficiencies of the vitamins C, D and folic acid, as well as vitamins B1 and A.

Psychosocial causes such as isolation, loneliness, or financial problems affect the nutrient intake of old people, as do medication, dental problems, gastrointestinal disorders and alcohol.

Psychosocial causes

Vitamin D deficiency is particularly widespread among the elderly. Osteoporosis, which is the depletion of the bone tissue, and decalcification of bone are a serious problem for old people, especially women. Many old people withdraw from other people more and more on account of their increasing frailty. This often means that they receive little or no sunlight, so the body has to get by without the vitamin D which is synthesised in the skin.

• People with diet-related illnesses and healthy individuals alike would be advised to make use of services offered by a number of consumer advisory services to work out their own individual eating schedule, in discussion with qualified dietary consultants.

Pregnant and breast-feeding women

Pregnant and breast-feeding women have an underlying problem: a considerably increased requirement for nutrients must be met from a relatively small extra energy requirement from the diet. This can be especially problematic in the case of vitamins B1, B6 and folic acid, where many people with normal consumption of these substances barely get the recommended amount.

Problem of folic acid

In a study in 2,000 pregnant women, 15% were found to have an inadequate intake of the vitamins B1, B2 and B6 during the last trimester of pregnancy. The situation with regard to folic acid was not investigated in this study, but today folic acid is known to be one of the vitamins which is especially critical during pregnancy. Basically, the requirement of all vitamins is elevated during pregnancy, although the vitamins C, B2 (niacin), B12 and E only rarely appear to be a problem, even during the last three months. ·

In mothers who breast-feed for long periods, the supply level of vitamins can decline rapidly if their intake is inadequate, especially if their vitamin reserves were already strained during the pregnancy. Those primarily affected are vitamins A, B6, C and folic acid.

• Pregnancy and breast-feeding are phases in which it is sensible to boost the vitamin intake with vitamin supplements. Your doctor can test your vitamin status, so that appropriate preparations can then be prescribed.

Babies and infants

Breast milk can supply a baby with all its nutrients

During the first four months, wholly breast-fed babies are adequately provided with all nutrients from the breast milk, provided that the mother herself has an adequate intake.

The exception to this is vitamin D. Today, rickets, previously a disease of the socially disadvantaged, can still affect children, even those of highly educated parents. It occurs in cases where, for either ideological or diet-related reasons, mothers are no longer giving their babies vitamin D supplements.

Deficiency phenomena can also occur if parents pass on their own bad eating habits to their children at an early stage. This applies as much to a poor diet with an excess of carbohydrates of low nutritional and physiological value, such as sugar and white flour, and an unnecessarily high animal-protein content, as to extreme alternative types of nutrition. Alternative diets are often highly unsuitable for children. For example a strictly macrobiotic diet can just as easily lead to severe deficiency phenomena in infants as can strict forms of vegetarianism.

Bad eating habits of the parents

• If the mother's own intake is good, the baby's will be good as well.

The socially disadvantaged

Our nutritional state, and therefore also our vitamin intake, reflect our niche in society. People who have to watch every penny they spend often scrimp on eating and may, in some circumstances, decline into a deficiency state. Studies of eating habits have clearly shown that higher earners also have a better vitamin intake.

Income and social status are therefore also crucial for our vitamin supply.

A representative study from the USA has shown that the vitamin A and vitamin C intakes of the wealthy classes in the USA are considerably higher than the corresponding vitamin intakes of the socially disadvantaged. The poorer classes consume about 40% less vitamins A and C than do higher earners. It is clear that this is largely due to the high price of fresh fruit and vegetables which are rich in vitamins A and C.

• It is especially important for people in financial difficulties to ensure they eat a healthy diet, because they need the strength and energy to break out of their situation. Dietary information services provided by consumer advisory groups can give hints and guidance on how to eat healthily for very little money.

Watch out for vitamin depleters

Living longer quite simply involves giving up habits which shorten the life span. Everyday habits like smoking, excessive alcohol consumption and constant stress not only endanger our health, but are also depleters of our vitamin supply and can lead to a considerable increase in our vitamin requirement. Many drugs are also vitamin depleters – the contraceptive pill is a prime example.

In the sections which follow, you will discover more about the individual factors and their destructive effect on vitamins. For each depleter, you will be given advice on how you can limit the vitamin deficit.

Smoking destroys vitamins

Smokers need more vitamins than non-smokers, the vitamin most likely to be at risk being vitamin C. In heavy smokers, the vitamin C concentration in the blood plasma is often less than half the average value of non-smokers. This increases the susceptibility of the body to infections, and the incidence of cancer may be increased because vitamin C is believed to have a direct detoxifying effect on certain constituents of cigarette smoke, for example cyanides, formaldehyde, carbon monoxide and nitrosamines.

Vitamin C is badly affected

Smoking also has a negative effect on the status of other water-soluble vitamins. Low values of the vitamins B2, B6, B12 and folic acid are often detected in the blood and tissue of smokers.

A study in the USA confirms the fear that young smokers are especially badly affected by this problem. It shows that the plasma ascorbic acid level of female adolescent smokers is on average 60% lower than the corresponding value in non-smokers. The researchers also discovered that, not only do smokers have an elevated vitamin requirement, they also feed themselves significantly less well than non-smokers.

The risk for young people is twice as great

• The more cigarettes smoked, the greater the decline in the vitamin C level. So smokers should have between 150-200% (150mg) of the RNI for vitamin C.

Alcohol poisons the vitamin supply

Alcoholics also have an increased vitamin requirement. As well as damaging the body by constantly poisoning it with alcohol, alcoholics usually eat irregularly and badly: calorie-rich alcoholic drinks (wine contains about 650kcal/l and beer about 500kcal/l) absolutely ruin the appetite. The calories in alcohol provide only 'empty' calories without any important nutrients. So alcoholics frequently suffer from pronounced vitamin deficiency. Vitamins B1, B2, niacin, B6 and folic acid are usually those most severely affected.

'Empty' calories

Vitamin deficiency due to heavy drinking manifests itself in a wide range of different symptoms: defects of stimulus conduction along the nerves are the typical signs of B1 and B6 deficiency, and anaemia in cases of folic acid deficiency. The skin and gastrointestinal tract of the alcoholic show all the symptoms of vitamin B2 and niacin deficiency. Alcohol and acetaldehyde, which is present in many alcoholic drinks, interfere above all with the metabolism of vitamin B6 in the liver. If cirrhosis of the liver is already present, the vitamin B6 metabolism can cease completely if the consumption of alcohol is continued.

Alcohol disturbs the vitamin B6 metabolism

Chronic alcohol consumption is also one of the main reasons for the prevalence of folic acid deficiency in the populations of industrialised countries and anaemia, common among alcoholics, is very often a consequence of deficiency of this vitamin.

The effective therapy is abstinence

The only effective therapy is abstinence. Until this can be achieved, however, the vitamin supply of the patient can often only be kept in order by taking a multivitamin preparation.

Stress uses up the body's reserves

Stress has come to be so much a feature of modern life as to be almost unavoidable. Routine stresses of everyday life are one of the most damaging influences on our health: among other effects they make massive demands on our vitamin intake, particularly on the vitamin C balance.

One of the most important stress regulators of the body is the adrenal cortex. In situations in which demands are excessive, the adrenal cortex produces adrenaline and other hormones for the regulation of stress, an activity which uses vitamin C. The relatively substantial quantity of stored vitamin C which the adrenal gland draws upon is, however, very rapidly exhausted in conditions of constant stress, and the stress-regulating organ must then rely on an increased and uninterrupted exogenous intake. People who continuously suffer from stress are frequently vulnerable to illness. The low vitamin C intake weakens the immune system which makes it difficult to fight infections.

Stress damages the health

It is assumed that, under conditions of severe stress, the vitamin E and vitamin B requirements are also elevated as a result of the onslaught which stress represents for the nervous system. Everyone who continuously suffers from stress should in particular ensure that their vitamin C intake is increased by eating large quantities of fresh fruit and vegetables. The daily eating plan should also contain foods with a high content of vitamins E and B (see vitamin table, pages 28 and 29).

Vitamins B, C and E are required for stress

Women on the pill need more vitamins

Ovulation inhibitors have always been the most reliable contraceptive, and a correspondingly large number of women take oestrogen-containing products daily. However, only a small minority of them know that oestrogens have a detrimental effect on the vitamin status.

An Australian study shows that no vitamin is entirely unaffected by oral contraceptives. The amino acid, tryptophan, is severely depleted in a process which depends upon an adequate supply of vitamin B6, thereby increasing the vitamin B6 requirement. Moreover, tryptophan is also the precursor of neurotransmitters, substances which are important for the disturbance-free coupling of our nerve cells. One of these neurotransmitters, serotonin, has a pronounced effect on mood. If we lack it, we react by becoming depressed. A vitamin B6 deficiency, and therefore disturbed tryptophan metabolism, can also increase pre-menstrual depression.

Folic acid, one of the problem vitamins, is adversely affected by the pill; ovulation inhibitors appear to impede the absorption of folic acid from the intestine.

The vitamin C requirement is increased because oestrogens activate an enzyme which converts vitamin C into an inactive form. The values for the vitamin B12 intake are sometimes very low in women taking the pill. It is, however, not yet known by what mechanism oestrogens upset the B12 metabolism.

Problems arise during pregnancy

The contraceptive-induced strain on the vitamin balance can become a problem if pregnancy occurs after years on the contraceptive. An underlying deficiency is a huge drawback during this period, in which the requirement is greatly increased; it endangers not only the health of the mother, but that of her baby as well.

Women who are unable to find an acceptable alternative to the contraceptive pill must be especially careful to ensure that they receive a healthy and nutritious diet, paying particular attention to their vitamin B6 and folic acid requirements. Besides many types of fish and green vegetables, the avocado is another good source; 150g of this fruit provides not only half the daily vitamin B6 requirement, but also just under a quarter of the folic acid requirement, as well as having a high content of vitamin E and pantothenic acid.

Harmful drug interactions

Antibiotics affect the balance of all vitamins

In many drug groups, interactions must be anticipated between the pharmaceutical substance and vitamins. If these drugs are taken for long periods, for example in cases of chronic disease, a considerably increased vitamin requirement may be required. The majority of active substances interact with several vitamins simultaneously. Antibiotic therapy, for example, affects the vitamin balance across almost the entire range. Relevant scientific knowledge is still very scanty. In by no means all cases do we know the effect of the particular active substance on the vitamin balance, and investigation of the effects on the vitamin status is unfortunately still not a compulsory part of clinical drug testing. The drugs which may influence the vitamin balance are shown in the table on page 97.

Sugar is naughty but nice

Sugar does not contain vitamins, but vitamins are required for its catabolism. Since vitamins, in particular vitamin B1, are eliminated via the kidneys instead of being stored, their reserves in the body are drastically reduced unless replenished from the diet. It is logical that, if a sugary diet is eaten, less will be ingested of other foods which could yield vitamins. A person who fills up with sweets often has very little appetite left for a meal which includes healthy foods such as salad, fresh fruit or vegetables. For this reason sugar, or a diet rich in sugar, can be a contributory factor in vitamin deficiency.

B1 supplies must be safeguarded

It is also worth remembering that by eating less sugar and fewer sweets we are not only protecting our vitamin reserves, but also preventing obesity and other negative consequences of an excess of sugary things such as tooth decay.

Drugs which may influence your vitamin balance

Drug group	Principal nutrients			Vitamins										Minerals										All nutrients
	Proteins	Fats	Carbohydrates	Vitamin B1	Vitamin B2	Vitamin B6	Vitamin B12	Folic acid	Vitamin C	Vitamin A	Vitamin D	Vitamin E	Vitamin K	Calcium	Iron	Fluoride	Iodine	Potassium	Copper	Magnesium	Sodium	Phosphorus	Zinc	
Analgesics, antirheumatics	●		●		●				●				●					●	●					
Appetite suppressants									●															●
Acid-binding and other drugs for gastric disorders				●					●					●	●	●			●		●	●		
Antibiotics		●			●	●	●	●	●	●			●	●	●			●			●		●	
Anticholinergics					●				●															●
Antidiabetics, oral	●		●			●								●										
Hypotensive drugs			●			●	●											●			●	●		
Anticonvulsants					●	●	●	●			●		●	●										
Digitalis glycosides														●				●				●		
Diuretics			●					●						●				●		●	●		●	
Glucocorticoids	●		●			●			●		●			●	●						●	●	●	
Contraceptive pill	●	●	●	●	●	●	●	●	●	●		●		●	●					●	●		●	
Laxatives	●	●	●							●	●	●	●	●				●						
Lipid-lowering drugs		●	●				●	●		●	●	●	●								●		●	
Psychoactive drugs – Neuroleptics									●					●				●		●				●
– Hypnotics	●								●	●	●			●								●		
Sulphonamides					●	●	●	●	●					●										
Tuberculosis drugs						●	●	●							●	●					●	●		
Uricosurics	●				●		●		●					●	●						●	●		

Vitamins for health every day

It all comes down to selecting the right foods

What people eat is food and meals, not vitamins, minerals and calories. Hardly anyone is prepared to keep a constant check on their vitamin intake with kitchen scales, nutrient table and pocket calculator.

Food should be varied and nutritious

If we eat a varied and nutritious diet, and do not fall into one of the high-risk groups, we are probably getting enough of all vitamins to safeguard our intake. But what do we mean by a 'varied' and 'nutritious' daily diet?

Eating the right foods

How can we be sure that we are eating the right mix of foods? For this, nutrition advisors have prepared practical guidelines which are easy to understand and put into practice. The foods we eat can be divided up into seven groups which form a 'diet circle'. By eating one or more of the foods in each of these seven groups each day we can safeguard our basic provision with all nutrients, not just vitamins but also minerals, trace elements, protein, carbohydrates and essential fatty acids.

Eat one complete diet circle every day

The seven food groups in the diet circle are:
1. Fruit
2. Vegetables, salad, potatoes
3. Bread, confectionery, cereal
4. Milk, cheese, dairy products
5. Meat, fish, eggs
6. Fat, oils, butter, margarine
7. Drinks

Fruit and vegetables are always good for the vitamin supply

Fruit and vegetables should never be absent from your daily eating schedule. These foods are best eaten raw as often as possible. No one who eats large quantities of fruit and vegetables need have any worries about his or her intake of provitamin A (beta-carotene), vitamin C, folic acid, vitamin K and vitamin B6. There are many ways in which fruit and vegetables can be incorporated into the daily diet: with an apple, pear, banana or berries in the morning cereal, by

Eat fruit and vegetables raw

mixing fruit and yoghurt for a mid-morning snack, with salad and vegetables as a side dish or as a main course for the midday meal, or with cold meats for supper.

You can supplement your vitamin reserves in a great many delicious and refreshing ways with freshly-pressed fruit or vegetable juice. Eat lots of potatoes because they contain all the vitamins, not just vitamins D and B12; their content of vitamin C, niacin, vitamin K and vitamin B1 is especially high.

Cereal produce supplies all the B-group vitamins

Bread, and other cereal products from the whole grain are some of our staple foods. They are important sources of the vitatmins B1, B2, B6, niacin, pantothenic acid and folic acid. The range of different breads which are available provides sufficient variety for bread never to become boring.

You should also eat regular meals of muesli with ground-up cereal or wholemeal cereal flakes containing wheat-germ, which is particularly rich in vitamin E and nutritious essential fatty acids.

Vitamin content of the whole wheat grain as compared with wheat flour: note the large losses

Vitamin	Whole grain	Household flour (type 405)	Loss
Carotene	0.23	0.06	74%
Thiamine (B1)	0.48	0.06	88%
Riboflavin (B2)	0.14	0.03	79%
Pyridoxine (B6)	0.44	0.18	59%
Folic acid	0.049	0.01	80%
Tocopherol (E)	3.2	2.3	28%

(Values are in mg per 100g)

Milk and milk produce are indispensable

Whole milk contains all the vitamins

Whole milk contains all the vitamins. Although some of these are present only in very small quantities (for example vitamin C), its vitamin content is sufficient to adequately nourish a newborn human or animal, which is dependent upon exogenous provision of nutrients. Milk is particularly important for our supply of vitamins A, B2 and B12; as little as half a pint a day safeguards the B12 intake, while cheese contains especially large amounts of vitamin A.

Milk and dairy produce are also very important because, as well as the vitamins, they contain a lot of calcium which is important for bones and teeth, and valuable protein

Meat, fish and eggs in the correct amounts

Meat is an important food

Total abstinence from meat is unnecessary. When eaten in moderation, good-quality meat is not just an important donor of proteins and minerals: it also contains a considerable number of vitamins. For example, it is one of the most important suppliers of the B-group vitamins, in particular vitamin B1. Offal, especially liver, is positively loaded with vitamins. However, since liver also contains considerable amounts of heavy metals, it should not be eaten more than once or twice a month.

For many reasons, fish should be served fairly frequently – if possible at least once a week. It is an excellent and usually low-calorie source of protein; salt-water fish contains large quantities of iodine, a trace element which many of us have in short supply, and also contribute good amounts of vitamins A, D, niacin and B6.

Eggs are a good source of the vitamins A, B2, B12 and biotin, although their high cholesterol content means that we should consume no more than one or two a week.

Fats and oils yield vitamins A and E

A healthy diet should contain butter as it has an excellent vitamin A content and contains some vitamin D, and cold-pressed vegetable oils, which make an important contribution to our vitamin E supply, as well as providing the vital unsaturated fatty acids.

Drink fruit and vegetable juices

Avoid fizzy drinks containing sugar and drink fresh fruit and vegetable juices. They contain a large proportion of the vitamins present in the food from which they originate. Juices are best diluted with mineral water, which provides important minerals.

A wholefood diet ensures a good nutritional balance

Food should be in an unrefined state

In accordance with guidelines for a nutritious diet, we should eat less fat and sugar and we should eat our foods in as unrefined a state as possible.

The reasoning behind this is sound: all processing and handling of foods leads to a loss of nutrients, especially vitamins. For example, when fruit is cut up or grated, a large quantity of vitamin C is destroyed.

The best way to get a good vitamin supply from a nutritious diet is to eat more fruit, vegetables and wholemeal products. Vegetables are the food type with the highest density of vitamins and minerals; in other words, vegetables contain more vitamins and minerals per 100 calories than any other food group. Because of the large contribution they make towards providing the crucial vitamins folic acid and B2, and their high fibre content, vegetables are of particular value for nutrition-related physiology. Pulses are the vegetable with the richest protein content, and in addition they contain decent amounts of the critical vitamins B1, B2, B6 and folic acid.

Healthy preparation techniques

Preparation: vitamins are sensitive

Food should be eaten as near to its natural state as is practical, and it should be treated with as much care as possible during its storage and preparation. If food has to be cooked it should be for the shortest possible time and at the lowest possible temperature. Vitamins are destroyed by too much heat or light. The following examples explain how vitamin losses can occur due to careless storage and preparation.

Keep cooking to a minimum

Correct storage is important

Storage

Fruit and vegetables are rarely eaten immediately after they are bought. But even a short period of time in the kitchen, or refrigerator reduces the vitamin C content of green vegetables. If spinach, salad, green beans or peas are stored for one day in the kitchen, they lose up to 40% of their vitamin C content. After two days, there may already be an 80% decline in the vitamin C content.

Washing

Vitamins are leached out by water

In order to prevent leaching of vitamins, fruit and vegetables should only be washed for a short time and before being cut into smaller pieces. Never allow leafy salad vegetables to stand in water for long periods: soaking for a quarter of an hour leads to the loss of between 20 and 30% of the vitamin C content, depending on the type of vegetable; after an hour, the losses are already more than doubled. The vitamin B1 content too may be reduced by 20%.

Cutting

Peeled apples or potatoes very rapidly turn brown on the surface. The smaller the pieces into which the fruit or vegetable has been cut, and the longer it is kept, the more vitamin C is lost. If spinach, tomatoes or bananas are left to stand after being cut into small pieces, about 10% of the vitamin is lost even after only a few minutes. After two hours at room temperature, a third of the vitamin may already have been lost. In the case of chopped white cabbage, red cabbage or Chinese leaves, the losses after storing for two hours may be as much as 60%.

Avoid peeling fruit and vegetables

Use lemon juice to protect vitamin C

To prevent these excessive losses of vitamin C, dribble a little vinegar or lemon juice on the freshly prepared food. This slows deterioration considerably.

Peeling

Wherever possible, leave fruit unpeeled and tomatoes unskinned, and boil potatoes in their skins – most of the vitamins are known to be present in and under the skin.

The vitamin C content of apples and pears is 10-15% higher in the skin than in the fleshy part of the fruit; the content of the vitamins niacin, folic acid and riboflavin is also higher in the skin. Tomatoes' skins contain higher concentrations of vitamin C, riboflavin, and niacin than the flesh.

Boiling, keeping warm

Cooking destroys vitamins

The boiling of vegetables reduces the vitamin C content by half, on average. Steaming is a more conservative process as only a quarter of the vitamin C is lost.

Another vitamin which is especially vulnerable to the adverse effects of cooking apart from vitamin C and thiamine (average losses due to boiling: 40%) is folic acid. When heated experimentally for two minutes, folic-acid losses of up to 80% were recorded. Longer periods of boiling and warming destroys the vitamin completely.

Keeping prepared food warm causes high losses of vitamins C, B1 and B2. If absolutely essential, it is better to reheat the food as less vitamin is lost.

The average losses of thiamine as a result of the boiling, steaming and braising of pork, beef or veal are in the region of 70%. When roasting, baking or grilling are used, one must still anticipate a thiamine loss of about 40%. The thiamine losses during the baking of bread are between 10 and 75%. However, the vitamin losses from cooking vegetables or meat in the microwave are often considerably lower than with conventional cooking.

Processed foods

The fact that these vitamin losses have not caused us all to be carried off by scurvy is partly thanks to the food industry. Food is now handled so professionally during industrial processing that vitamin losses are usually lower than during the preparation of food in the home. Who would have thought that massive-scale sterilization and pasteurization of foods would lead to less nutrient being lost than when food is prepared in the home? Sterilization by heating at high temperatures for short periods is still the most conservative method for heating heat-sensitive vitamins.

Ultra-high temperature heating

Milk is a good example. Pasteurization (pasteurized whole milk) and ultra-high heating (UHT milk) leave the vitamin A content of the milk almost unchanged, and reduce the B-group vitamins by only around 5% to a maximum of 20%. Only with heating for longer periods, for example in the case of sterilized UHT milk, are the vitamin losses greater: vitamin B12 is almost totally destroyed, and the content of other vitamins may be reduced by up to 50%.

Sterilizing, pasteurizing

With knowledge of precisely where vitamins are destroyed or lost, losses can be reduced by careful preparation and storage.

Prevent vitamin loss in the kitchen

The method of cultivation appears to have hardly any effect on the vitamin content of fruit and vegetables, although the quantity of toxins contained in produce grown using some "alternative" methods of cultivation may be less than that associated with conventional cultivation.

Position and soil type, time of harvesting, degree of ripeness and climatic conditions during growth do, however, exert a considerable influence on the vitamin content of vegetable produce.

Fruit and vegetables should be used on the day of purchase if at all possible. Even in the vegetable drawer in the refrigerator, lettuce in particular loses considerable quantities of vitamin C. Asparagus, fungi, broccoli and strawberries all lose their vitamins very quickly.

Buy vegetables whole. For example, don't have the stalk removed from cabbage, or the leaves from carrots. If stored under optimal conditions, the leaves of cabbage and cauliflower produce vitamin C for up to nine days after harvesting, which they then transport into the edible parts.

Do not leave freshly-purchased vegetables and fruit lying around for unnecessarily long periods of time unpackaged and in warm places.

Fresh products can be kept for longer by freezing immediately after purchase. Deep-freezing is the best way of preserving vitamins and other nutrients. Blanch vegetables before freezing, by immersing them in hot water for a short time. This inactivates certain enzymes (ascorbic-acid oxidases) which normally degrade vitamin C during storage.

Protect unpackaged fruit and vegetables, milk and vegetable oils from light. In vegetable oils, vitamin E in particular is susceptible to the influence of light.

Health and enjoyment of food

Recipe ideas for vitamin-rich cuisine

There is no art to eating vitamin-rich food, as long as a few basic rules are followed.

Every time we drink fruit and vegetable juices we give ourselves a small shot of vitamins. Juicing retains almost the entire vitamin and mineral content and liquid fruit and vegetables contain all the vitamins the body requires for health.

An improvement in the vitamin supply can also be achieved by tasty additions to the diet, such as orange or blackcurrant juice to boost the vitamin-C reserves, vegetable juice for the folic acid supply or carrot juice to boost the carotene levels.

Pure fruit juices have a 100% fruit content from concentrate or juice. In fruit-juice drinks the fruit content is limited to around 30% as a flavouring additive. Diet fruit juices are sweetened with sugar substitutes and contain about 50% fewer calories than comparable juices. Before buying fruit or vegetable drinks to boost your vitamin intake you should check the label to ensure that they are completely pure and not diluted.

From drinking to eating: you can ensure that you get the full vitamin content of fruit and vegetables, as well as all other important nutrients, by eating them raw, and by eating salads. To give you an idea of how delicious and varied vitamin-rich food can be, here are a few sample recipes which can be varied, dressed and seasoned to taste.

Chicory and orange salad

with a sauce consisting of quark, honey and lemon juice, garnished with flaked and roasted almonds.
Particularly rich in vitamin C.

Apple and celery salad

Grate the apple and celery, mix with rings of leek, and dress with a sauce of soured cream, lemon juice, olive oil, a little horseradish and herbs.
Good vitamin E and C content.

Spinach salad with chick-peas and soya beans

Mix spinach and sprouts with softened and germinated chick-peas. Garnish with onion rings, and prepare with a dressing made from vinegar, puréed garlic, salt, pepper and cold-pressed oil.
Absolutely loaded with folic acid, not least of all on account of the high folic-acid content of the chick-peas.

Fennel and carrot salad

Cut the fennel into strips and the carrots into sticks, mix with finely chopped spring onions and add a dressing made of lemon juice, oil, salt and pepper.
Rich in carotene and vitamin C.

Spoil yourself with vitamins for a whole day!

Breakfast: crunchy muesli

2 heaped dessertspoons rolled oats,
1 pear (or alternatively one fruit of your choice),
* 1 teaspoon wheat-germ, 1 teaspoon chopped hazelnuts,*
*   1 beaker whole-milk yoghurt, a little fresh whole milk*
      Preparation: Peel the pear and cut into pieces, or grate
      and mix with the other ingredients. For a super-high
      dose of vitamins C, B1 and E.
      Eat with a glass of fruit juice or a cup of aromatic coffee.

Coffee-break snack

1 piece of fresh fruit,
Natural or fruit yoghurt,
Wholewheat biscuits or a crispbread, covered with banana,
quark, gherkin or tomato

Midday meal – Fish in mustard sauce

125g potatoes, 150g carrots, herb salt,
175g white fish fillets, 1 dessertspoon lemon juice,
150ml yeast extract and vegetable stock,
2 dessertspoons (40g) soured cream,
2 teaspoons moderately hot mustard, pepper,
1 teaspoon (5g) oil
Preparation: Boil the potatoes in their skins, and cut the
carrots into strips. Boil in a very small quantity of salted
water for 8 minutes. Sprinkle the fillets with lemon juice.
Simmer in the stock for about 8 minutes. Stir together the
soured cream and mustard, heat gently, season with salt
and pepper. Sprinkle parsley over the vegetables and the
peeled potatoes. Place fillet on top and pour on sauce.
Eat with a previously prepared chicory salad with sweetcorn
and a tangy roquefort dressing. For dessert, quark with fruit.

The starter yields folic acid, the carrots folic acid, and the fish provides vitamins D, E and niacin. The quark provides vitamin B12.

An energy-giving snack in the afternoon

1 muesli bar,
or 1 slice of wholemeal cake

Dinner – simple yet imaginative

Serve wholemeal bread as a vitamin-rich accompaniment to an imaginatively created cold salad.
Here are a few ideas:
Kiwi fruit and rice salad,
Orange and rolled fillet of ham,
Tangy pasta salad with apple, orange and pineapple,
Paprika and sweetcorn salad with cooked ham,
Make a dressing made from vinegar, oil and herbs.
Eat with fruit or vegetable juice, or a spritzer (fruit juice with mineral water).

Vitamin-rich nightcap

Fruit cocktail
A healthy menu like this can be repeated in many different variations. With the basic knowledge provided in this book and by taking an interest in eating well and healthily, you can banish boredom from your dinner plate by serving up a varied and vitamin-rich diet.

Vitamins for fitness, health and beauty
by Dr Friedhelm Mühleib
Published originally under the title "Fit, schön & gesund –
Vitamine" by Gräfe und Unzer Verlag GmbH, Munich
© 1994 Gräfe und Unzer

Authorized English language edition published by
Time-Life Books BV, 1066 Amsterdam
© 1997 Time-Life Books BV
First English language printing 1997

English translation by Carmona UK
Editorial Manager: Christine Noble
Editor: Alison Mackonochie
Edit: Mark Stephenson
Layout/DTP: Dawn McGinn

ISBN 0 7054 3511 3

20 19 18 17 16 15 14 13 12 11 10 9 8 7 6 5 4 3 2 1